CHINESE
Your Favorite Restaurant Recipes

pil

Publications International, Ltd.

Front cover photography by Getty Images and Publications International, Ltd.

Photography on pages 4, 5, 6, 8, 10, 12, 14, 16, 17, 18, 20, 21, 22, 24, 26, 27, 28, 29, 30, 32, 34, 36, 38, 40, 42, 43, 44, 46, 48, 50, 51, 78, 79, 80, 82, 84, 85, 86, 87, 88, 90, 91, 92, 94, 96, 98, 99, 100, 102, 103, 104, 106, 107, 108, 110, 111, 112, 113, 114, 116, 118, 120, 121, 122, 124, 125, 144, 146, 148, 149, 150, 152, 153, 154, 156, 157, 158, 160, 161, 162, 164, 165, 166, 168, 170, 171, 172, 173, 174, 176, 178, 179, 180, 182, 184 and 186 by Shutterstock.

Some of the products listed in this publication may be in limited distribution.

Pictured on the front cover: Savory Pork Stir-Fry *(page 52)*.
Pictured on the back cover *(clockwise from top left):* Orange Beef *(page 66),* Mini Egg Rolls *(page 8)* and Wonton Soup *(page 42)*.

ISBN-13: 978-1-4508-1166-8
ISBN-10: 1-4508-1166-3

Library of Congress Control Number: 2009940311

Manufactured in China.

8 7 6 5 4 3 2 1

Microwave Cooking: Microwave ovens vary in wattage. Use the cooking times as guidelines and check for doneness before adding more time.

Preparation/Cooking Times: Preparation times are based on the approximate amount of time required to assemble the recipe before cooking, baking, chilling or serving. These times include preparation steps such as measuring, chopping and mixing. The fact that some preparations and cooking can be done simultaneously is taken into account. Preparation of optional ingredients and serving suggestions is not included.

Publications International, Ltd.

Table of
CONTENTS

Menu

Fan-Tailed Chinese Shrimp

Mini Egg Rolls

Soy-Braised Chicken Wings

Crab Cakes Canton

Ginger Plum Spareribs

Steamed Pork Wontons with
Sweet Soy Dipping Sauce

Sweet and Sour Pork Meatballs

Shrimp Toast

Baked Egg Rolls

Sweet-Hot Orange Chicken
Drumettes

Baked Crab Rangoon

Pot Stickers

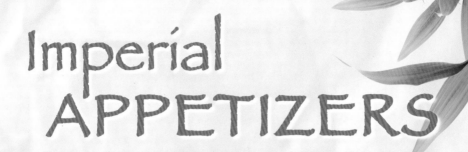

Imperial
APPETIZERS

Steamed Pork Wontons with
Sweet Soy Dipping Sauce, page 16

Fan-Tailed Chinese Shrimp

1 tablespoon seasoned rice vinegar
1 tablespoon oyster sauce
1 tablespoon soy sauce
2 cloves garlic, minced
¼ teaspoon red pepper flakes
18 large raw shrimp (about 1 pound), peeled and deveined, tails intact
1 tablespoon peanut or canola oil
¼ cup chopped fresh cilantro
    Plum sauce or sweet and sour sauce (optional)

1. For marinade, combine vinegar, oyster sauce, soy sauce, garlic and red pepper flakes in large nonreactive bowl; mix well.

2. To butterfly shrimp, use small sharp knife to cut back of each shrimp three fourths of the way through. Open shrimp; place cut side down on work surface, pressing to flatten into butterfly shape. Add shrimp to bowl with marinade; toss to coat. Cover and refrigerate at least 30 minutes or up to 2 hours.

3. Heat oil in large nonstick skillet over medium-high heat. Remove shrimp from marinade; discard marinade. Cook shrimp (in batches if necessary) 3 to 4 minutes or until pink and opaque, turning once. Transfer to serving platter; sprinkle with cilantro. Serve with plum sauce for dipping, if desired. *Makes 6 servings*

Mini Egg Rolls

½ **pound ground pork**
3 **cloves garlic, minced**
1 **teaspoon minced fresh ginger**
¼ **teaspoon red pepper flakes**
6 **cups (12 ounces) shredded coleslaw mix**
¼ **cup soy sauce**
1 **tablespoon cornstarch**
1 **tablespoon seasoned rice vinegar**
½ **cup chopped green onions**
28 **wonton wrappers**
    Peanut or canola oil for frying
    Sweet and sour sauce and Chinese hot mustard

1. Cook and stir pork, garlic, ginger and red pepper flakes in large nonstick skillet over medium heat about 4 minutes or until pork is cooked through, stirring to break up meat. Add coleslaw mix; cover and cook 2 minutes.

2. Combine soy sauce and cornstarch in small bowl; mix well. Stir into pork mixture. Add vinegar; cook 2 to 3 minutes or until sauce thickens. Remove from heat; stir in green onions.

3. Place one wonton wrapper on clean work surface with one point facing you. Spoon 1 level tablespoon pork mixture across and just below center of wrapper. Fold bottom point of wrapper up over filling; fold side points over filling, forming envelope shape. Moisten inside edges of top point with water and roll egg roll toward top point, pressing firmly to seal. Repeat with remaining wrappers and filling.

4. Heat about ¼ inch oil in large skillet over medium heat; fry egg rolls in small batches about 2 minutes per side or until golden brown. Drain on paper towels. Serve warm with sweet and sour sauce and hot mustard for dipping. *Makes 28 mini egg rolls*

Soy-Braised Chicken Wings

¼ **cup dry sherry**

¼ **cup soy sauce**

3 **tablespoons sugar**

2 **tablespoons cornstarch**

2 **tablespoons minced garlic, divided**

2 **teaspoons red pepper flakes**

12 **chicken wings (about 2½ pounds), tips removed and
       cut into halves**

2 **tablespoons vegetable oil**

3 **green onions, cut into 1-inch pieces**

¼ **cup chicken broth**

1 **teaspoon sesame oil**

1 **tablespoon sesame seeds, toasted**

**To toast sesame seeds, place in small skillet. Shake skillet over medium-low heat about
3 minutes or until seeds begin to pop and turn golden. Remove from heat.*

1. For marinade, combine sherry, soy sauce, sugar, cornstarch,
1 tablespoon garlic and red pepper flakes in large bowl; mix well.
Reserve ¼ cup marinade. Add chicken wings to remaining marinade;
cover and refrigerate overnight, turning once or twice.

2. Drain wings; discard marinade. Heat oil in wok over high heat; add
half of wings. Cook 5 to 10 minutes or until wings are brown on all sides,
turning occasionally. Remove with slotted spoon to bowl. Repeat with
remaining 1 tablespoon vegetable oil and wings.

3. Add remaining 1 tablespoon garlic and green onions to wok; cook
and stir 30 seconds. Add wings and broth. Cover; cook and stir 5 to
10 minutes or until wings are cooked through.

4. Add sesame oil to reserved marinade; mix well. Pour over wings in
wok; cook and stir 2 minutes or until wings are glazed. Transfer to serving
platter; sprinkle with sesame seeds.   *Makes 2 dozen wings*

Crab Cakes Canton

7 ounces fresh, frozen or pasteurized crabmeat or imitation crabmeat
1½ cups fresh whole wheat bread crumbs
¼ cup thinly sliced green onions
1 clove garlic, minced
1 teaspoon minced fresh ginger
2 egg whites, lightly beaten
1 tablespoon teriyaki sauce
2 teaspoons vegetable oil, divided
Prepared sweet and sour sauce (optional)

1. Pick out and discard any shell or cartilage from crabmeat. Combine crabmeat, bread crumbs, onions, garlic and ginger in medium bowl; mix well. Add egg whites and teriyaki sauce; mix well. Shape into patties about ½ inch thick and 2 inches in diameter.*

2. Heat 1 teaspoon oil in large nonstick skillet over medium heat. Add half of crab cakes to skillet; cook 2 minutes per side or until golden brown. Remove to serving plate; keep warm. Repeat with remaining 1 teaspoon oil and crab cakes. Serve with sweet and sour sauce for dipping, if desired. *Makes 12 cakes*

Crab cakes may be made ahead to this point; cover and refrigerate up to 24 hours before cooking.

tip

To make fresh bread crumbs, remove the crusts from fresh or day-old bread slices. Then process in a food processor using an on/off pulsing action until crumbs are of the desired size.

Ginger Plum Spareribs

1 jar (10 ounces) damson plum preserves or apple jelly
¹⁄₃ cup KARO® Light or Dark Corn Syrup
¹⁄₃ cup soy sauce
¹⁄₄ cup chopped green onions
2 cloves garlic, minced
2 teaspoons ground ginger
2 pounds pork spareribs, trimmed, cut into serving pieces

1. In small saucepan, combine preserves, corn syrup, soy sauce, green onions, garlic and ginger. Stirring constantly, cook over medium heat until melted and smooth.

2. Pour into 11×7×2-inch baking dish. Add ribs, turning to coat. Cover; refrigerate several hours or overnight, turning once.

3. Remove ribs from marinade; place on rack in shallow baking pan.

4. Bake in 350°F oven about 1 hour or until tender, turning occasionally and basting with marinade. Do not baste during last 5 minutes of cooking.   *Makes about 20 appetizer or 4 main-dish servings*

Ginger Plum Chicken Wings: Omit spareribs. Follow recipe for Ginger Plum Spareribs. Use 2½ pounds chicken wings, separated at the joints (tips discarded). Bake 45 minutes, basting with marinade during last 30 minutes.

Prep Time: 15 minutes, plus marinating
Bake Time: 1 hour

Steamed Pork Wontons with Sweet Soy Dipping Sauce

Wontons

    8 ounces lean ground pork

    ¼ cup chopped fresh cilantro

    1½ tablespoons grated fresh ginger

    1 teaspoon grated orange peel

    ¼ teaspoon ground red pepper

    ⅛ teaspoon salt

    24 wonton wrappers

    3 teaspoons vegetable oil

    1 cup water

Dipping Sauce

    3 tablespoons water

    2 tablespoons sugar

    2 tablespoons white vinegar

    2 tablespoons lime juice

    2 tablespoons soy sauce

1. Combine pork, cilantro, ginger, orange peel, red pepper and salt in medium bowl. Place rounded teaspoon in center of each wonton wrapper. Fold up edges, using small amount of water to seal.

2. Heat 1½ teaspoons oil in large nonstick skillet over medium-high heat. Add 12 wontons and cook 1 minute or until golden brown on bottom. Add ½ cup water; cover and cook 5 minutes or until water has evaporated. Place on serving platter and cover with foil to keep warm. Repeat with remaining oil, wontons and water.

3. Combine sauce ingredients in small bowl. Microwave sauce on HIGH 20 to 30 seconds. *Makes 8 servings*

Sweet and Sour Pork Meatballs

 1 pound ground pork
 ¼ cup finely chopped water chestnuts
 ¼ cup chopped onion
 1 egg, lightly beaten
 ¼ cup soy sauce, divided
 ⅛ teaspoon ground ginger
 1 teaspoon vegetable oil
 1 can (8 ounces) pineapple chunks
 1 tablespoon vinegar
 1 tablespoon cornstarch
 1 tablespoon sugar

In large bowl, combine pork, water chestnuts, onion, egg, 2 tablespoons soy sauce and ginger; shape into 1-inch balls. In nonstick skillet cook meatballs in hot oil until browned. Remove meatballs and drain on paper towels, reserving drippings in skillet.

Drain pineapple, reserving juice. In 1-cup measure combine pineapple juice, remaining 2 tablespoons soy sauce and vinegar. Add water to equal 1 cup liquid. In mixing bowl combine cornstarch and sugar. Gradually stir in pineapple juice mixture; mix well. Add juice mixture to pan drippings. Cook over medium heat until thickened and bubbly, stirring constantly. Stir in meatballs and reserved pineapple chunks. Cook 4 to 5 minutes or until heated through.   *Makes 24 meatballs*

Prep Time: 25 minutes

Favorite recipe from **National Pork Board**

Shrimp Toast

12 large raw shrimp, peeled and deveined, tails intact
1 egg
2 tablespoons plus 1½ teaspoons cornstarch
¼ teaspoon salt
   Dash black pepper
3 slices white sandwich bread, each cut into 4 triangles
1 hard-cooked egg yolk, cut into ½-inch pieces
1 slice (1 ounce) cooked ham, cut into ½-inch pieces
1 green onion, finely chopped
   Vegetable oil for frying

1. Cut deep slit down back of each shrimp; press gently with fingers to flatten.

2. Beat egg, cornstarch, salt and pepper in large bowl until blended. Add shrimp; toss to coat well.

3. Drain each shrimp and press, cut side down, onto each piece of bread. Brush small amount of leftover egg mixture onto each shrimp.

4. Place 1 piece each hard-cooked egg yolk and ham and scant ¼ teaspoon green onion on top of each shrimp.

5. Heat about 1 inch oil in wok or large skillet over medium-high heat to 375°F. Add three or four bread pieces at a time; cook 1 to 2 minutes, spooning hot oil over shrimp until cooked through and toast is golden brown. Drain on paper towels. *Makes 12 servings*

Baked Egg Rolls

Sesame Dipping Sauce (recipe follows)
1 ounce dried shiitake mushrooms
1 large carrot, shredded
1 can (8 ounces) sliced water chestnuts, drained and minced
3 green onions, minced
3 tablespoons chopped fresh cilantro
12 ounces ground chicken
2 tablespoons minced fresh ginger
6 cloves garlic, minced
2 tablespoons soy sauce
2 teaspoons water
1 teaspoon cornstarch
12 egg roll wrappers
1 tablespoon vegetable oil
1 teaspoon sesame seeds

1. Prepare Sesame Dipping Sauce; set aside.

2. Place mushrooms in small bowl. Cover with warm water; let stand 30 minutes or until tender. Rinse well; drain, squeezing out excess water. Cut off and discard stems; finely chop caps. Combine mushrooms, carrot, water chestnuts, green onions and cilantro in large bowl.

3. Spray medium nonstick skillet with nonstick cooking spray; heat over medium-high heat. Brown chicken 2 minutes, stirring to break up meat. Add ginger and garlic; cook and stir 2 minutes or until chicken is cooked through. Add to mushroom mixture. Sprinkle with soy sauce; mix thoroughly.

4. Preheat oven to 425°F. Spray baking sheet with cooking spray; set aside. Blend water into cornstarch in small bowl. Lay 1 wrapper on work surface. Spoon about ⅓ cup filling across center of wrapper to within about ½ inch of sides. Fold bottom of wrapper over filling. Fold in sides. Brush ½-inch strip across top edge with cornstarch mixture; roll up and seal. Place seam side down on baking sheet. Repeat with remaining wrappers.

5. Brush egg rolls with oil. Sprinkle with sesame seeds. Bake 18 minutes or until golden and crisp. Serve with Sesame Dipping Sauce.

Makes 6 servings

Sesame Dipping Sauce

¼ **cup rice vinegar**
4 **teaspoons soy sauce**
2 **teaspoons minced fresh ginger**
1 **teaspoon dark sesame oil**

Combine all ingredients in small bowl; blend well.

Makes about ½ cup

Sweet-Hot Orange Chicken Drumettes

¼ **cup plus 3 tablespoons orange juice, divided**
4 **tablespoons orange marmalade or apricot jam, divided**
3 **tablespoons hoisin sauce**
1 **teaspoon grated fresh ginger**
10 **chicken drumettes (about 1¼ pounds)**
3 **tablespoons chili garlic sauce**
¼ **teaspoon salt**
¼ **teaspoon red pepper flakes**
⅛ **teaspoon five-spice powder (optional)**
⅛ **teaspoon black pepper**
   Sesame seeds (optional)

1. Preheat oven to 400°F. Line baking sheet with heavy-duty foil; generously spray foil with nonstick cooking spray.

2. Combine ¼ cup orange juice, 2 tablespoons orange marmalade, hoisin sauce and ginger in medium microwavable bowl. Microwave on HIGH 1 minute or until marmalade melts; stir until well blended.

3. Dip drumettes, one at a time, in orange juice mixture; place on prepared baking sheet. Bake 15 minutes; turn and bake 10 minutes or until drumettes are golden brown and cooked through.

4. Meanwhile, combine remaining 3 tablespoons orange juice, 2 tablespoons orange marmalade, chili garlic sauce, salt, red pepper flakes, five-spice powder, if desired, and black pepper in small microwavable bowl. Microwave on HIGH 1 minute or until marmalade melts; stir until well blended.

5. To serve, arrange drumettes on platter. Garnish with sesame seeds; serve with dipping sauce.   *Makes about 5 servings*

Baked Crab Rangoon

1 can (6 ounces) white crabmeat, drained, flaked

4 ounces (½ of 8-ounce package) PHILADELPHIA® Neufchâtel Cheese, ⅓ Less Fat than Cream Cheese, softened

¼ cup thinly sliced green onions

¼ cup KRAFT® Mayo Light Mayonnaise

12 wonton wrappers

PREHEAT oven to 350°F. Mix crabmeat, Neufchâtel cheese, onions and mayonnaise.

SPRAY 12 (2½-inch) muffin cups with cooking spray. Gently place 1 wonton wrapper in each cup, allowing edges of wrappers to extend above sides of cups. Fill evenly with crabmeat mixture.

BAKE 18 to 20 minutes or until edges are golden brown and filling is heated through. Serve warm. Garnish with sliced green onions, if desired.

Makes 12 servings, 1 wonton each

Food Facts: Wonton wrappers are usually found in the grocery store in the refrigerated section of the produce department.

Mini Crab Rangoon: Use 24 wonton wrappers. Gently place 1 wonton wrapper in each of 24 miniature muffin cups sprayed with cooking spray. Fill evenly with crabmeat mixture and bake as directed. Makes 12 servings, 2 appetizers each.

Prep Time: 20 minutes
Bake Time: 20 minutes

Pot Stickers

2 cups all-purpose flour
¾ cup plus 2 tablespoons boiling water
½ cup very finely chopped napa cabbage
8 ounces lean ground pork
2 tablespoons finely chopped water chestnuts
1 green onion, finely chopped
1½ teaspoons cornstarch
1½ teaspoons dry sherry
1½ teaspoons soy sauce
½ teaspoon minced fresh ginger
½ teaspoon dark sesame oil
¼ teaspoon sugar
2 tablespoons vegetable oil, divided
⅔ cup chicken broth, divided
Soy sauce, vinegar and chili oil

1. Place flour in large bowl; make well in center. Pour in boiling water; stir with wooden spoon until dough forms.

2. On lightly floured surface, knead dough until smooth and satiny, about 5 minutes. Cover dough; let rest 30 minutes.

3. Squeeze cabbage to remove as much moisture as possible; place in large bowl. Add pork, water chestnuts, green onion, cornstarch, sherry, soy sauce, ginger, sesame oil and sugar; mix well.

4. Divide dough into two equal portions; cover one portion with plastic wrap while working with other portion. On lightly floured surface, roll out dough to ⅛-inch thickness. Cut out 3-inch circles with round cookie cutter.

5. Place 1 rounded teaspoon filling in center of each dough circle. To shape each pot sticker, lightly moisten edges of one dough circle with

water; fold in half. Starting at one end, pinch edges together making four pleats along edge; set dumpling down firmly, seam side up. Cover finished dumplings while shaping remaining dumplings. (Dumplings may be refrigerated for up to 4 hours or frozen in large resealable food storage bag.)

6. To cook dumplings, heat 1 tablespoon vegetable oil in large nonstick skillet over medium heat. Place half of pot stickers in skillet, seam side up. (If cooking frozen dumplings, do not thaw.) Cook 5 to 6 minutes or until bottoms are golden brown.

7. Pour in ⅓ cup broth; cover. Reduce heat to low. Simmer until all liquid is absorbed, about 10 minutes (15 minutes if frozen). Repeat with remaining vegetable oil, dumplings and broth. Serve with soy sauce, vinegar and chili oil for dipping.   *Makes about 3 dozen*

Menu

Egg Drop Soup

Tofu and Snow Pea Noodle Bowl

Canton Pork Stew

Hot and Sour Soup

Ming Dynasty Beef Stew

Chinese Chicken Stew

Wonton Soup

Beef Soup with Noodles

Spinach Noodle Bowl with Ginger

Oriental Fish Stew

Quick Hot and Sour Chicken Soup

Soups
& MORE

Wonton Soup, page 42

Egg Drop Soup

4 cups chicken broth
2 tablespoons soy sauce
1 tablespoon dry sherry
1 tablespoon cold water
1 tablespoon cornstarch
2 eggs, well beaten
2 green onions, thinly sliced
2 teaspoons dark sesame oil

1. Combine broth, soy sauce and sherry in large saucepan; bring to a boil over high heat. Reduce heat to low; simmer 2 minutes.

2. Stir water into cornstarch in small bowl; mix well. Stir mixture into soup; simmer 2 to 3 minutes or until slightly thickened.

3. Stirring constantly in one direction, slowly add beaten eggs to soup in thin stream. Stir in green onions. Remove from heat; stir in sesame oil.

Makes 4 servings

tip

An extremely important seasoning in all Asian cuisines, soy sauce was developed more than 3,000 years ago. There are many brands and varieties, so choose one that suits your taste.

Tofu and Snow Pea Noodle Bowl

5 cups water
6 tablespoons chicken broth powder*
4 ounces uncooked vermicelli, broken in thirds
1 cup shredded carrots
½ pound firm tofu, rinsed, patted dry and cut in ¼-inch cubes
3 ounces snow peas
½ teaspoon chili garlic sauce
½ cup chopped green onions
¼ cup chopped fresh cilantro (optional)
2 tablespoons lime juice
1 tablespoon grated fresh ginger
2 teaspoons soy sauce

*Chicken-flavored vegetarian broth powder can be found in natural food stores and some supermarkets.

1. Bring water to a boil in large saucepan over high heat. Stir in broth powder and vermicelli. Return to a boil. Reduce heat to medium-high; simmer 6 minutes. Stir in carrots, tofu, snow peas and chili garlic sauce; simmer 2 minutes.

2. Remove from heat; stir in green onions, cilantro, if desired, lime juice, ginger and soy sauce.   *Makes 4 servings*

Tip: For a vegetarian soup, substitute 5 cups of canned vegetable broth for the water and broth powder.

Canton Pork Stew

1½ pounds boneless lean pork shoulder or pork loin roast, cut into
   1-inch pieces
1 teaspoon ground ginger
¼ teaspoon ground cinnamon
¼ teaspoon ground red pepper
1 tablespoon peanut or vegetable oil
1 large onion, coarsely chopped
3 cloves garlic, minced
1 can (about 14 ounces) chicken broth
¼ cup dry sherry
1 package (about 10 ounces) frozen baby carrots, thawed
1 large green bell pepper, cut into 1-inch pieces
3 tablespoons soy sauce
1½ tablespoons cornstarch
   Cilantro (optional)

1. Sprinkle pork with ginger, cinnamon and red pepper; toss well. Heat oil in large saucepan or Dutch oven over medium-high heat.

2. Add pork to saucepan; brown on all sides. Add onion and garlic; cook and stir 2 minutes. Add broth and sherry; bring to a boil over high heat. Reduce heat to medium-low. Cover and simmer 40 minutes.

3. Stir in carrots and green pepper; cover and simmer 10 minutes or until pork is fork-tender. Blend soy sauce into cornstarch in cup until smooth. Stir into stew; cook and stir 1 minute or until stew boils and thickens. Garnish with cilantro.   *Makes 6 servings*

Hot and Sour Soup

1 package (1 ounce) dried shiitake mushrooms
4 ounces firm tofu, drained
4 cups chicken broth
3 tablespoons white vinegar
2 tablespoons soy sauce
½ to 1 teaspoon hot chili oil
¼ teaspoon white pepper
1 cup shredded cooked pork, chicken or turkey
½ cup drained canned bamboo shoots, cut into thin strips
3 tablespoons water
2 tablespoons cornstarch
1 egg white, lightly beaten
¼ cup thinly sliced green onions or chopped fresh cilantro
1 teaspoon dark sesame oil

1. Place mushrooms in small bowl; cover with warm water. Soak 20 minutes to soften. Drain; squeeze out excess water. Discard stems; slice caps. Press tofu lightly between paper towels; cut into ½-inch cubes.

2. Combine broth, vinegar, soy sauce, chili oil and white pepper in medium saucepan. Bring to a boil over high heat. Reduce heat to medium and simmer 2 minutes.

3. Stir in mushrooms, tofu, pork and bamboo shoots; heat through.

4. Blend water into cornstarch in small bowl until smooth. Stir into soup; cook and stir 4 minutes or until soup boils and thickens. Remove from heat.

5. Stirring constantly in one direction, slowly pour egg white in thin stream. Stir in green onions and sesame oil.   *Makes 4 to 6 servings*

Ming Dynasty Beef Stew

**2 pounds boneless beef chuck or veal shoulder, cut into
   1½-inch pieces**
1 teaspoon Chinese five-spice powder*
½ teaspoon red pepper flakes
2 tablespoons peanut or vegetable oil, divided
1 large onion, coarsely chopped
2 cloves garlic, minced
1 cup beef broth
1 cup beer
2 tablespoons soy sauce
1 tablespoon cornstarch
   Hot cooked Chinese rice noodles
   **Grated lemon peel, chopped fresh cilantro and/or chopped
   peanuts (optional)**

*Chinese five-spice powder is a blend of cinnamon, cloves, fennel seed, anise and
Szechuan peppercorns. It is available in most supermarkets and at Asian grocery stores.*

1. Sprinkle beef with five-spice powder and red pepper flakes. Heat
1 tablespoon oil in large saucepan or Dutch oven over medium-high
heat. Add half of beef; brown on all sides. Remove to plate. Repeat
with remaining oil and beef.

2. Add onion and garlic to saucepan; cook and stir 3 minutes. Add
broth and beer; bring to a boil. Reduce heat. Return beef along with any
accumulated juices to saucepan; cover and simmer 1 hour 15 minutes or
until beef is fork-tender.*

3. Blend soy sauce into cornstarch in cup until smooth. Stir into saucepan.
Cook and stir uncovered, 2 minutes or until mixture thickens. Serve over
noodles. Garnish with lemon peel, cilantro and peanuts.

Makes 6 to 8 servings

*Stew may be oven-braised if saucepan or Dutch oven is ovenproof. Cover and bake in
350°F oven 1 hour 15 minutes or until beef is fork-tender. Proceed as directed in step 3.*

Chinese Chicken Stew

1 pound boneless skinless chicken thighs, cut into 1-inch pieces
1 teaspoon Chinese five-spice powder
½ to ¾ teaspoon red pepper flakes
1 tablespoon peanut or vegetable oil
1 onion, coarsely chopped
1 package (8 ounces) fresh mushrooms, sliced
2 cloves garlic, minced
1 can (about 14 ounces) chicken broth, divided
1 tablespoon cornstarch
1 red bell pepper, cut into ¾-inch pieces
2 tablespoons soy sauce
2 green onions, cut into ½-inch pieces
1 tablespoon sesame oil
3 cups hot cooked white rice
¼ cup coarsely chopped fresh cilantro

Slow Cooker Directions

1. Toss chicken with five-spice powder and red pepper flakes in small bowl. Heat peanut oil in large skillet. Add onion and chicken; cook and stir about 5 minutes or until chicken is browned. Add mushrooms and garlic; cook and stir until chicken is cooked through.

2. Combine ¼ cup broth and cornstarch in small bowl; set aside. Place cooked chicken mixture, remaining broth, bell pepper and soy sauce in slow cooker. Cover; cook on LOW 3½ hours or until peppers are tender.

3. Stir in cornstarch mixture, green onions and sesame oil. Cook, uncovered, 30 to 45 minutes or until juices have thickened. Serve with rice and sprinkle with cilantro. *Makes 6 servings*

Wonton Soup

¼ **pound ground pork, chicken or turkey**
¼ **cup finely chopped water chestnuts**
2 **tablespoons soy sauce, divided**
1 **egg white, lightly beaten**
1 **teaspoon minced fresh ginger**
12 **wonton wrappers**
6 **cups chicken broth**
1½ **cups spinach, torn**
1 **cup thinly sliced cooked pork (optional)**
½ **cup diagonally sliced green onions**
1 **tablespoon dark sesame oil**
Shredded carrot (optional)

1. For wonton filling, combine ground pork, water chestnuts,
1 tablespoon soy sauce, egg white and ginger in small bowl; mix well.

2. Place 1 wonton wrapper with point toward edge of counter. Mound
1 teaspoon filling near bottom point. Fold bottom point over filling, then
roll wrapper over once. Moisten inside points with water. Bring side
points together below the filling, overlapping slightly; press together
firmly to seal. Repeat with remaining wrappers and filling.* Keep finished
wontons covered with plastic wrap while filling remaining wrappers.

3. Combine broth and remaining 1 tablespoon soy sauce in large
saucepan. Bring to a boil over high heat. Reduce heat to medium;
add wontons. Simmer, uncovered, 4 minutes or until filling is cooked
through.

4. Stir in spinach, sliced pork, if desired, and green onions; remove from
heat. Stir in sesame oil; garnish with shredded carrot.

Makes 2 servings

**Wontons may be made ahead to this point; cover and refrigerate up to 8 hours or
freeze up to 3 months. Proceed as directed above if using refrigerated wontons; increase
simmering time to 6 minutes if using frozen wontons.*

Beef Soup with Noodles

2 tablespoons soy sauce
1 teaspoon minced fresh ginger
¼ teaspoon red pepper flakes
1 boneless beef top sirloin steak (about ¾ pound)
1 tablespoon peanut or vegetable oil
2 cups sliced fresh mushrooms
2 cans (about 14 ounces each) beef broth
3 ounces (1 cup) fresh snow peas, cut diagonally into 1-inch pieces
1½ cups hot cooked egg noodles (2 ounces uncooked)
1 green onion, cut diagonally into thin slices
1 teaspoon dark sesame oil (optional)
  Red bell pepper strips (optional)

1. Combine soy sauce, ginger and red pepper flakes in small bowl. Spread mixture evenly over both sides of steak. Marinate 15 minutes.

2. Heat peanut oil in large deep skillet over medium-high heat. Drain steak; reserve marinade. Add steak to skillet; cook 5 minutes per side. Let stand on cutting board 10 minutes.

3. Add mushrooms to skillet; stir-fry 2 minutes. Add broth, snow peas and reserved marinade, scraping up browned bits; bring to a boil. Reduce heat to medium-low. Stir in noodles.

4. Cut steak lengthwise in half, then crosswise into thin slices. Stir into soup; heat through. Stir in green onion and sesame oil. Garnish with red pepper strips.   *Makes 4 main-dish or 6 appetizer servings*

Spinach Noodle Bowl with Ginger

1 can (48 ounces) chicken broth (about 6 cups)
4 ounces uncooked dry vermicelli noodles, broken into thirds
1½ cups matchstick carrots
3 ounces snow peas, cut in half and stems removed
4 cups packed spinach leaves (4 ounces)
1½ cups diced cooked shrimp or chicken
½ cup finely chopped green onions
1 tablespoon grated fresh ginger
1 teaspoon soy sauce
⅛ to ¼ teaspoon red pepper flakes

1. Bring broth to a boil in Dutch oven over high heat. Add vermicelli; return to a boil. Cook until al dente, about 2 minutes less than package instructions. Add carrots and snow peas; cook 2 minutes or until pasta is tender.

2. Remove from heat; stir in spinach, shrimp, green onions, ginger, soy sauce and red pepper flakes. Let stand 2 minutes to absorb flavors before serving. *Makes 4 servings*

tip

Keep a couple bags of cooked shrimp in the freezer for quick additions to soups, stir-fries and pasta dishes. To thaw quickly, place frozen shrimp in a bowl of cool water 10 minutes; drain shrimp.

Oriental Fish Stew

8 to 10 dried shiitake mushrooms
¼ cup soy sauce
2 tablespoons rice wine
1 teaspoon chopped fresh ginger
½ pound medium shrimp, peeled and deveined
½ pound halibut, cubed
1 tablespoon vegetable oil
2 cups diagonally sliced bok choy
1½ cups diagonally sliced napa cabbage
1 cup broccoli florets
2 cloves garlic, chopped
2 cubes vegetable bouillon dissolved in 2 cups hot water
½ cup bottled clam juice or water
2 tablespoons *each* cornstarch and cold water
¼ pound pea pods, stems removed
2 green onions with tops, sliced
Hot cooked rice (optional)

1. Soften mushrooms in bowl of warm water 15 minutes; drain. Discard stems; slice caps. Set aside. Combine soy sauce, rice wine and ginger in medium bowl. Add shrimp and halibut; marinate 10 minutes.

2. Heat oil in 5-quart Dutch oven over medium-high heat; cook and stir bok choy, napa cabbage, broccoli and garlic 3 minutes.

3. Drain seafood, reserving marinade. Add dissolved vegetable bouillon, clam juice and seafood marinade to Dutch oven. Bring to a boil. Reduce heat; simmer 5 to 10 minutes. Add seafood and mushrooms; simmer 3 to 5 minutes or until shrimp are opaque and fish flakes easily when tested with fork.

4. Blend cornstarch and water until smooth; add to stew. Cook and stir until stew boils and thickens slightly. Remove from heat; stir in pea pods and green onions. Serve over rice, if desired.   *Makes 4 to 6 servings*

Quick Hot and Sour Chicken Soup

2 cups water

2 cups chicken broth

1 package (about 10 ounces) refrigerated fully cooked chicken breast strips, cut into pieces

1 package (about 7 ounces) chicken-flavored rice and vermicelli mix

1 jalapeño pepper,* minced

2 green onions, chopped

1 tablespoon soy sauce

1 tablespoon lime juice

1 tablespoon minced fresh cilantro

*Jalapeño peppers can sting and irritate the skin, so wear rubber gloves when handling peppers and do not touch your eyes.

1. Combine water, broth, chicken, rice mix, jalapeño, green onions and soy sauce in large saucepan; bring to a boil over high heat. Reduce heat to low. Cover; simmer 20 minutes or until rice is tender, stirring occasionally.

2. Stir in lime juice; sprinkle with cilantro.   *Makes 4 servings*

Menu

SAVORY PORK STIR-FRY

HOISIN BEEF STIR-FRY

ASIAN PORK RIBS WITH SPICY NOODLES

CHINESE PEPPERCORN BEEF

SZECHUAN PORK STIR-FRY OVER SPINACH

SPICY CHINESE PEPPER STEAK

GARLIC BEEF

MANDARIN PORK STIR-FRY

ONE PAN PORK FU YUNG

ORANGE BEEF

LEMON-ORANGE GLAZED RIBS

STIR-FRIED MU SHU PORK WRAPS

CASHEW BEEF

SESAME BEEF WITH PINEAPPLE-PLUM SAUCE

CHINESE PORK & VEGETABLE STIR-FRY

BEEF AND ASPARAGUS STIR-FRY

Beef
& PORK

Orange Beef, page 66

Beef & PORK

Savory Pork Stir-Fry

1 pound lean boneless pork loin
1 tablespoon vinegar
1 tablespoon soy sauce
1 teaspoon sesame oil
1 clove garlic, minced
½ teaspoon ground ginger
1 teaspoon vegetable oil
1 (10-ounce) package frozen stir-fry vegetables, unthawed
1 tablespoon chicken broth or water
Hot cooked rice (optional)
1 tablespoon toasted sesame seeds (optional)

Slice pork across grain into ⅛-inch strips. Marinate in vinegar, soy sauce, sesame oil, garlic and ginger for 10 minutes. Heat vegetable oil in nonstick pan until hot. Add pork mixture and stir-fry for 3 to 5 minutes, until pork is no longer pink. Add vegetables and chicken broth. Stir mixture, cover and steam until vegetables are crisp-tender. Serve over hot cooked rice and sprinkle with toasted sesame seeds, if desired.

Makes 4 servings

Prep Time: 20 minutes

Favorite recipe from **National Pork Board**

Beef & PORK

Hoisin Beef Stir-Fry

   1 teaspoon grated orange peel
   ⅓ cup orange juice
   3 tablespoons hoisin sauce
   1 tablespoon cider vinegar
   ¼ teaspoon red pepper flakes
   ¼ cup almond slivers
   ½ teaspoon dark sesame oil
   1 medium red bell pepper, sliced
   4 cups shredded coleslaw mix
   ¼ teaspoon salt
 1½ cups fresh or thawed frozen snow peas
  12 ounces beef tip sirloin steak, cut into thin strips

1. Combine orange peel, juice, hoisin sauce, vinegar and red pepper flakes in small bowl.

2. Heat large nonstick skillet over medium-high heat. Add almonds; cook 2 minutes or until beginning to brown. Remove from skillet; set aside.

3. Add sesame oil to skillet; swirl to coat. Add pepper; cook and stir 2 minutes. Add coleslaw and salt; cook and stir 2 minutes. Remove to serving platter.

4. Add snow peas to skillet; cook and stir 2 minutes or until crisp-tender. Place over coleslaw mixture. Cover; keep warm.

5. Add beef to skillet; cook and stir 2 minutes. Arrange over vegetables. Cover; keep warm.

6. Add hoisin mixture to skillet; cook and stir 2 minutes. Spoon sauce evenly over beef. Sprinkle with almonds.   *Makes 4 servings*

Asian Pork Ribs with Spicy Noodles

1 can (about 14 ounces) beef broth

½ cup water

¼ cup rice wine vinegar

1 tablespoon grated fresh ginger

1 cup (about 1 ounce) dried sliced shiitake mushrooms

¼ teaspoon red pepper flakes

1 tablespoon Chinese five-spice powder

1 tablespoon dark sesame oil

1 teaspoon ground ginger

1 teaspoon chili powder

2 full racks pork back ribs (about 4 pounds)

¾ cup hoisin sauce, divided

1 pound (16 ounces) thin spaghetti, cooked according to package directions

¼ cup thinly sliced green onions

¼ cup chopped fresh cilantro

Slow Cooker Directions

1. Stir together broth, water, vinegar, grated ginger, mushrooms and red pepper flakes in 6-quart slow cooker.

2. Combine five-spice powder, sesame oil, ground ginger and chili powder to form paste. Cut rib racks in half; blot dry with paper towels. Rub all surfaces with spice paste; brush with half of hoisin sauce.

3. Place ribs in slow cooker with broth mixture (do not stir). Cover and cook on LOW 8 to 10 hours or on HIGH 5 to 6 hours or until meat is fork-tender. Remove ribs to platter; brush lightly with remaining hoisin sauce. Cover; keep warm. Skim off any fat from cooking liquid.

4. Place warm spaghetti in shallow bowls. Ladle some cooking liquid over spaghetti; sprinkle with green onions and cilantro. Slice ribs; serve over pasta. *Makes 4 servings*

Chinese Peppercorn Beef

2 teaspoons whole black and pink peppercorns*

2 teaspoons coriander seeds

1 tablespoon peanut or canola oil

1 boneless beef top sirloin steak, about 1¼ inches thick (1½ pounds)

2 teaspoons dark sesame oil

½ cup thinly sliced shallots or sweet onion

½ cup chicken broth

2 tablespoons soy sauce

1 tablespoon dry sherry

1 tablespoon cold water

1 teaspoon cornstarch

2 tablespoons thinly sliced green onion or chopped fresh cilantro

*You may use all black peppercorns, if preferred.

1. Place peppercorns and coriander seeds in small resealable food storage bag; seal bag. Coarsely crush spices using meat mallet or bottom of heavy saucepan. Brush peanut oil over both sides of steak; sprinkle with peppercorn mixture, pressing lightly.

2. Heat large heavy skillet over medium-high heat. Add steak; cook 4 minutes or until seared on bottom, without turning. Reduce heat to medium; turn steak and continue cooking 3 to 4 minutes for medium-rare or until desired doneness. Transfer steak to cutting board; tent with foil.

3. Add sesame oil to same skillet; heat over medium heat. Add shallots; cook and stir 3 minutes. Add broth, soy sauce and sherry; simmer 2 minutes.

4. Stir water into cornstarch in small bowl; mix well. Add to skillet; cook and stir 3 to 4 minutes or until sauce thickens. Carve steak crosswise into thin slices. Spoon sauce over steak; sprinkle with green onion.

Makes 4 servings

Chinese Peppercorn Beef

Beef & PORK

Szechuan Pork Stir-Fry over Spinach

 2 teaspoons dark sesame oil, divided
¾ cup matchstick-size carrot strips
½ pound pork tenderloin, cut into thin strips
 3 cloves garlic, minced
 2 teaspoons minced fresh ginger
¼ to ½ teaspoon red pepper flakes
 1 tablespoon soy sauce
 1 tablespoon dry sherry
 2 teaspoons cornstarch
 8 ounces baby spinach
 2 teaspoons sesame seeds, toasted*

To toast sesame seeds, spread in small skillet. Shake skillet over medium-low heat about 3 minutes or until seeds begin to pop and turn golden. Remove from heat.

1. Heat 1 teaspoon oil in large nonstick skillet over medium-high heat. Add carrot strips; cook and stir 3 minutes. Add pork, garlic, ginger and red pepper flakes; stir-fry 3 minutes or until pork is barely pink in center.

2. Combine soy sauce, sherry and cornstarch in small bowl until well blended. Add to pork mixture; stir-fry about 1 minute or until sauce thickens.

3. Heat remaining 1 teaspoon oil in medium saucepan over medium-high heat. Add spinach; cover and cook 1 minute or until spinach is barely wilted. Transfer spinach to 2 serving plates. Spoon pork mixture over spinach. Sprinkle with sesame seeds. *Makes 2 servings*

Spicy Chinese Pepper Steak

**1 (1-pound) boneless beef top sirloin steak or tenderloin tips, cut
into thin strips**
1 tablespoon cornstarch
3 cloves garlic, minced
½ teaspoon red pepper flakes
2 tablespoons peanut or canola oil, divided
1 green bell pepper, cut into thin strips
1 red bell pepper, cut into thin strips
¼ cup oyster sauce
2 tablespoons soy sauce
3 tablespoons chopped fresh cilantro or green onions

1. Combine beef, cornstarch, garlic and red pepper flakes in medium
bowl; toss to coat.

2. Heat 1 tablespoon oil in wok or large skillet over medium-high heat.
Add bell peppers; stir-fry 3 minutes. Transfer peppers to small bowl; set
aside. Add remaining 1 tablespoon oil and beef mixture to skillet; stir-fry
4 to 5 minutes or until beef is barely pink in center.

3. Add oyster sauce and soy sauce to skillet; stir-fry 1 minute. Return
peppers to skillet; stir-fry 1 to 2 minutes or until sauce thickens. Sprinkle
with cilantro just before serving.   *Makes 4 servings*

Garlic Beef

1 teaspoon sesame oil
1 pound beef eye of round, trimmed of fat, cut into thin strips
1 package (10 ounces) frozen chopped broccoli
1 tablespoon minced garlic
1 tablespoons soy sauce
¼ teaspoon black pepper

Heat oil in 12-inch nonstick skillet over high heat. Add beef, broccoli, garlic, soy sauce and black pepper. Cook and stir 15 minutes or until beef is cooked through. *Makes 4 servings*

Mandarin Pork Stir-Fry

1½ cups DOLE® Pineapple Orange or Pineapple Juice, divided
    Vegetable cooking spray
12 ounces lean pork tenderloin, chicken breast or turkey tenderloin, cut into thin strips
1 tablespoon finely chopped fresh ginger *or* ½ teaspoon ground ginger
2 cups shredded DOLE® Carrots
½ cup chopped DOLE® Pitted Prunes or Chopped Dates
4 green onions, cut into 1-inch pieces
2 tablespoons low-sodium soy sauce
1 teaspoon cornstarch

• Heat 2 tablespoons juice over medium-high heat in large nonstick skillet sprayed with vegetable cooking spray until juice bubbles.

• Add pork and ginger; cook and stir 3 minutes or until pork is no longer pink. Remove pork from skillet.

• Heat 3 more tablespoons juice in skillet; add carrots, prunes and green onions. Cook and stir 3 minutes.

• Stir soy sauce and cornstarch into remaining juice; add to carrot mixture. Stir in pork; cover and cook 2 minutes or until heated through.
Makes 4 servings

Prep Time: 15 minutes
Cook Time: 15 minutes

One Pan Pork Fu Yung

1 cup chicken broth
1 tablespoon cornstarch
½ teaspoon dark sesame oil, divided
2 teaspoons canola oil
½ pound boneless pork tenderloin, chopped
4 tablespoons sliced green onions, divided
1 cup sliced mushrooms
¼ teaspoon salt
¼ teaspoon white pepper
1 cup bean sprouts
2 eggs
2 egg whites

1. Combine broth, cornstarch and ¼ teaspoon sesame oil in small saucepan. Cook and stir over medium heat about 5 to 6 minutes or until sauce thickens.

2. Heat canola oil in 12-inch nonstick skillet over medium-high heat. Add pork; stir-fry about 4 minutes or until no longer pink.

3. Add mushrooms, 2 tablespoons green onions, remaining ¼ teaspoon sesame oil, salt and pepper to skillet; stir-fry 4 to 5 minutes or until mushrooms are lightly browned. Add sprouts; stir-fry 1 minute. With spatula, flatten mixture in skillet.

4. Beat eggs and egg whites in medium bowl; pour over pork mixture. Reduce heat to low. Cover; cook about 3 minutes or until eggs are set.

5. Cut pork fu yung into 4 wedges. Top each wedge with ¼ cup sauce and sprinkle with remaining 2 tablespoons green onion.

Makes 4 servings

Orange Beef

1 pound boneless beef top sirloin or tenderloin steaks
2 cloves garlic, minced
1 teaspoon grated orange peel
2 tablespoons soy sauce
2 tablespoons orange juice
1 tablespoon dry sherry
1 tablespoon cornstarch
1 tablespoon peanut or vegetable oil
2 cups hot cooked rice (optional)
Orange peel strips or orange slices (optional)

1. Cut beef in half lengthwise, then cut crosswise into thin slices. Toss with garlic and orange peel in medium bowl.

2. Blend soy sauce, orange juice and sherry into cornstarch in cup until smooth.

3. Heat oil in wok or large skillet over medium-high heat; stir-fry beef in batches 2 to 3 minutes or until barely pink in center. Stir soy sauce mixture and add to wok. Cook and stir 30 seconds or until sauce boils and thickens. Serve over rice, if desired; garnish with orange peel strips.

Makes 4 servings

Lemon-Orange Glazed Ribs

2 whole slabs baby back pork ribs, cut into halves (about 3 pounds)
2 tablespoons soy sauce
2 tablespoons orange juice
2 tablespoons fresh lemon juice
2 cloves garlic, minced
¼ cup orange marmalade
1 tablespoon hoisin sauce

1. Place ribs in large resealable food storage bag. Combine soy sauce, juices and garlic in small bowl; pour over ribs. Close bag securely; turn to coat. Marinate in refrigerator at least 4 hours or up to 24 hours, turning occasionally.

2. Preheat oven to 350°F. Drain ribs; reserve marinade. Place ribs on rack in foil-lined, shallow roasting pan. Brush half of marinade evenly over ribs; bake 20 minutes. Turn ribs over; brush with remaining marinade. Bake 20 minutes.

3. Remove ribs from oven; pour off drippings. Combine marmalade and hoisin sauce in cup; brush half of mixture over ribs. Return to oven; bake 10 minutes or until glazed. Turn ribs over; brush with remaining marmalade mixture. Bake 10 minutes more or until ribs are browned and glazed.   *Makes 4 servings*

Stir-Fried Mu Shu Pork Wraps

1 tablespoon dark sesame oil

1 red bell pepper, cut into thin strips

1 small pork tenderloin (¾ pound), cut into strips

1 medium zucchini or summer squash, cut into bite-size pieces

3 cloves garlic, minced

2 cups coleslaw mix or shredded cabbage

2 tablespoons hoisin sauce

4 (10-inch) flour tortillas

¼ cup plum sauce

1. Heat oil in large deep nonstick skillet over medium-high heat. Add bell pepper; cook and stir 2 minutes. Add pork, zucchini and garlic; cook and stir 4 to 5 minutes or until pork is cooked through and vegetables are crisp-tender. Add coleslaw mix; cook and stir 2 minutes or until wilted. Add hoisin sauce; cook and stir 1 minute.

2. Heat wraps according to package directions. Spread plum sauce down centers of wraps; top with pork mixture. Roll up tightly; cut diagonally in half. *Makes 4 servings*

Beef & PORK

Cashew Beef

- 2 tablespoons cooking oil
- 8 ounces beef (flank steak, skirt steak, top sirloin or filet mignon), cut into strips ¼ inch thick
- 3 tablespoons LEE KUM KEE® Premium Brand, Panda Brand or Choy Sun Oyster Sauce
- ¼ cup *each* red and green bell pepper strips (1-inch strips)
- 2 stalks celery, cut into ½-inch slices
- ½ cup carrot slices (½-inch slices)
- ¼ cup small button mushroom halves
- 2 tablespoons LEE KUM KEE® Soy Sauce
- 1 green onion, chopped
- 2 tablespoons cashews, toasted*
- 1 tablespoon LEE KUM KEE® Chili Garlic Sauce or Sriracha Chili Sauce

Cashews can be toasted in wok or skillet prior to cooking.

1. Heat wok or skillet over high heat until hot. Add oil, beef and LEE KUM KEE Oyster Sauce; cook until beef is half done.

2. Add bell peppers, celery, carrots, mushrooms and LEE KUM KEE Soy Sauce; stir-fry until vegetables are crisp-tender. Stir in green onion and cashews. Add LEE KUM KEE Chili Garlic Sauce or Sriracha Chili Sauce for spiciness or use as dipping sauce. *Makes 2 servings*

Sesame Beef with Pineapple-Plum Sauce

    3 tablespoons soy sauce, divided
3½ teaspoons cornstarch, divided
    1 pound beef flank steak, cut into thin slices
    2 teaspoons grated fresh ginger
    2 cloves garlic, minced
    ⅛ teaspoon red pepper flakes
    1 package (12 ounces) pineapple chunks
    1 tablespoon sesame seeds*
    1 tablespoon vegetable oil
    ¼ cup chicken broth
    ¼ cup minced green onions, plus additional for garnish
    ¼ cup thin red bell pepper slices
    2 tablespoons plum sauce
       Hot cooked noodles

To toast sesame seeds, spread in small skillet. Shake skillet over medium-low heat about 3 minutes or until seeds begin to pop and turn golden. Remove from heat.

1. Stir 2 tablespoons soy sauce into 1½ teaspoons cornstarch in medium bowl until well blended. Add steak, ginger, garlic and red pepper flakes; toss to coat. Let stand 30 minutes.

2. Drain pineapple, reserving juice.

3. Heat oil in large heavy skillet over medium-high heat. Working in batches, brown beef 2 minutes per side or until barely pink in center.

4. Stir 2 tablespoons pineapple juice into remaining 2 teaspoons cornstarch in small bowl. Add to skillet with broth, ¼ cup green onions, bell pepper, plum sauce and remaining 1 tablespoon soy sauce; cook and stir 1 minute or until sauce thickens. Add pineapple chunks; cook and stir until heated through. Sprinkle with sesame seeds and green onions. Serve over noodles.   *Makes 4 servings*

Chinese Pork & Vegetable Stir-Fry

2 tablespoons BERTOLLI® Olive Oil, divided
1 pound pork tenderloin or boneless beef sirloin, cut into
¼-inch slices
6 cups assorted fresh vegetables*
1 can (8 ounces) sliced water chestnuts, drained
1 envelope LIPTON® RECIPE SECRETS® Onion Soup Mix
¾ cup water
½ cup orange juice
1 tablespoon soy sauce
¼ teaspoon garlic powder

*Use any combination of the following: broccoli florets, thinly sliced red or green bell peppers, snow peas or thinly sliced carrots.

1. In 12-inch skillet, heat 1 tablespoon olive oil over medium-high heat; brown pork. Remove and set aside.

2. In same skillet, heat remaining 1 tablespoon olive oil and cook assorted fresh vegetables, stirring occasionally, 5 minutes. Stir in water chestnuts, soup mix blended with water, orange juice, soy sauce and garlic powder. Bring to a boil over high heat. Reduce heat to low and simmer, uncovered, 3 minutes. Return pork to skillet and cook 1 minute or until heated through.   *Makes about 4 servings*

Tip: Pick up pre-sliced vegetables from your local salad bar.

Beef and Asparagus Stir-Fry

¾ **cup water**

3 **tablespoons soy sauce**

3 **tablespoons hoisin sauce**

1 **tablespoon cornstarch**

1 **tablespoon peanut or vegetable oil**

1 **pound beef top sirloin, cut into thin strips**

1 **teaspoon dark sesame oil**

8 **shiitake mushrooms, stems removed and thinly sliced**

1 **cup baby corn**

8 **ounces asparagus (8 to 10 medium spears), cut into 1-inch pieces**

1 **cup sugar snap peas or snow peas**

½ **cup red bell pepper strips**

½ **cup cherry tomato halves (optional)**

   Hot cooked rice (optional)

1. Whisk water, soy sauce, hoisin sauce and cornstarch in small bowl; set aside.

2. Heat peanut oil in wok or large skillet over medium-high heat. Add beef; cook and stir 5 to 6 minutes or until still slightly pink. Remove beef to plate with slotted spoon.

3. Add sesame oil, mushrooms and baby corn to skillet; cook and stir 2 to 3 minutes or until mushrooms are tender and corn is heated through. Add asparagus, snap peas and bell peppers; cook and stir 1 minute or until crisp-tender.

4. Return beef and any accumulated juices to skillet. Stir reserved soy sauce mixture; add to skillet with tomatoes, if desired. Cook and stir 1 minute or until heated through and sauce is thickened. Serve with rice, if desired. *Makes 4 servings*

Menu

Sweet and Sour
Chicken

Ginger Plum Chicken

Chicken with Lychees

Cashew Chicken

Chicken and
Vegetables with
Mustard Sauce

Chinese Take-Out
Style Chicken and
Broccoli

Sweet 'n Sour

Spicy Orange
Chicken

Kung Po Chicken

Moo Goo Gai Pan

Pineapple-Hoisin
Hens

Twice-Fried Chicken
Thighs with Plum
Sauce

Sesame Chicken

Chicken
DELIGHTS

Sweet 'n Sour, page 90

Sweet and Sour Chicken

2 tablespoons unseasoned rice vinegar

3 cloves garlic, minced

2 tablespoons soy sauce

½ teaspoon minced fresh ginger

¼ teaspoon red pepper flakes (optional)

6 ounces boneless skinless chicken breasts

1 teaspoon vegetable oil

1 large green bell pepper, cut into 1-inch squares

3 green onions, cut into 1-inch pieces

1 tablespoon cornstarch

½ cup chicken broth

2 tablespoons apricot fruit spread

1 can (11 ounces) mandarin orange segments, drained

2 cups hot cooked white rice or Chinese egg noodles

1. Combine vinegar, garlic, soy sauce, ginger and red pepper flakes, if desired, in medium bowl. Cut chicken into ½-inch strips; toss with vinegar mixture. Marinate 20 minutes at room temperature.

2. Heat oil in wok or large nonstick skillet over medium heat. Drain chicken; reserve marinade. Add chicken to wok; stir-fry 3 minutes. Stir in bell pepper and green onions.

3. Stir cornstarch into reserved marinade. Stir broth, fruit spread and marinade mixture into wok. Cook and stir until chicken is cooked through and sauce is thickened. Add orange segments; stir until heated through. Serve over rice.

Makes 4 servings

Ginger Plum Chicken

2 tablespoons oil

1 tablespoon thinly sliced fresh ginger

8 ounces chicken (boneless breast or thigh), cut into 1-inch pieces

3 tablespoons LEE KUM KEE® Premium Brand or Panda Brand or Choy Sun Oyster Sauce

½ red bell pepper, cut into 1-inch pieces

½ green bell pepper, cut into 1-inch pieces

1 carrot, cut into 1-inch strips

3 tablespoons LEE KUM KEE® Plum Sauce

1 green onion, chopped

Hot cooked noodles

1. Heat oil in wok or skillet until hot. Add ginger; stir-fry 30 seconds. Add chicken and LEE KUM KEE Oyster Sauce; stir-fry until chicken is almost done.

2. Add bell peppers and carrot; stir-fry 1 to 2 minutes. Add LEE KUM KEE Plum Sauce and green onion; stir-fry until chicken is cooked through. Serve over noodles.   *Makes 2 servings*

Prep Time: 20 minutes
Cook Time: 10 to 12 minutes

tip

Store fresh unpeeled ginger tightly wrapped in the refrigerator for up to 2 weeks. Rinse and scrub outer skin before peeling with a sharp knife or vegetable peeler. Thinly slice, mince or grate ginger according to the recipe.

Chicken with Lychees

¼ cup plus 1 teaspoon cornstarch, divided
1 pound boneless skinless chicken breasts, cut into bite-size pieces
½ cup water, divided
½ cup tomato sauce
1 teaspoon sugar
1 teaspoon chicken bouillon granules
3 tablespoons vegetable oil
6 green onions, cut into 1-inch pieces
1 red bell pepper, cut into 1-inch pieces
1 can (11 ounces) whole peeled lychees, drained
Cooked Cellophane Noodles (recipe follows, optional)

1. Place ¼ cup cornstarch in large resealable food storage bag; add chicken. Seal bag; shake until chicken is well coated.

2. Combine remaining 1 teaspoon cornstarch and ¼ cup water in small cup; mix well. Combine remaining ¼ cup water, tomato sauce, sugar and bouillon granules in small bowl; mix well.

3. Heat oil in wok or large skillet over high heat. Add chicken; stir-fry 3 to 5 minutes or until lightly browned. Add green onions and bell pepper; stir-fry 1 minute.

4. Add tomato sauce mixture and lychees to wok. Reduce heat to low; cover and simmer 5 minutes or until chicken is cooked through.

5. Stir cornstarch mixture; add to wok. Cook and stir until sauce boils and thickens. Serve over hot Cellophane Noodles.   *Makes 4 servings*

Cellophane Noodles

8 ounces cellophane noodles (bean threads)
Vegetable oil for frying

1. Cut bundle of cellophane noodles in half. Gently pull each half apart into small bunches.

2. Heat oil in wok or large skillet over medium-high heat to 375°F. Using slotted spoon or tongs, lower small bunch of noodles into hot oil.

3. Cook 3 to 5 seconds or until noodles rise to top; remove immediately. Drain on paper towels. Repeat with remaining bunches.

Makes about 4 servings

Cashew Chicken

1 pound boneless skinless chicken breasts or thighs
2 teaspoons minced fresh ginger
1 tablespoon peanut or vegetable oil
1 medium red bell pepper, cut into short, thin strips
⅓ cup teriyaki sauce
⅓ cup roasted or dry roasted cashews
Hot cooked rice (optional)
Coarsely chopped fresh cilantro (optional)

1. Cut chicken into ½-inch slices; cut each slice into 1½-inch strips. Toss chicken with ginger in small bowl.

2. Heat oil in wok or large skillet over medium-high heat. Add chicken mixture; stir-fry 2 minutes. Add bell pepper; stir-fry 4 minutes or until chicken is cooked through.

3. Add teriyaki sauce; stir-fry 1 minute or until sauce is heated through. Stir in cashews. Serve over rice, if desired. Garnish with cilantro.

Makes 4 servings

Chicken and Vegetables with Mustard Sauce

1 tablespoon sugar

2 teaspoons cornstarch

2 teaspoons dry mustard

3 tablespoons soy sauce

2 tablespoons water

2 tablespoons rice vinegar

2 tablespoons vegetable oil, divided

1 pound boneless skinless chicken breasts, cut into 1-inch pieces

2 cloves garlic, minced

1 small red bell pepper, cut into thin slices

½ cup thinly sliced celery

1 small onion, cut into thin wedges

Chinese egg noodles

Fresh chives (optional)

1. Combine sugar, cornstarch and mustard in small bowl. Stir soy sauce, water and vinegar into cornstarch mixture until smooth; set aside.

2. Heat 1 tablespoon oil in wok over medium heat 2 minutes. Add chicken and garlic; stir-fry 5 to 6 minutes or until chicken is cooked through. Remove chicken to large bowl.

3. Drizzle remaining 1 tablespoon oil into wok and heat 30 seconds. Add pepper, celery and onion; stir-fry 3 minutes or until vegetables are crisp-tender.

4. Stir soy sauce mixture; add to wok. Stir-fry 30 seconds or until sauce boils and thickens.

5. Return chicken and any accumulated juices to wok; cook until heated through. Serve with noodles. Garnish with fresh chives.

Makes 4 servings

Chinese Take-Out Style Chicken and Broccoli

   2 cloves garlic, minced
   1 tablespoon grated fresh ginger
   1/8 teaspoon red pepper flakes
 12 ounces boneless skinless chicken breasts, cut into 2-inch pieces
   1 ounce unsalted peanuts or almond slivers
   2 teaspoons canola oil, divided
   1 medium onion, cut into 1/2-inch wedges
   1 medium carrot, thinly sliced
   2 cups broccoli florets (about 1-inch pieces)
1 1/4 cups chicken broth, divided
   1 tablespoon cornstarch
   2 garlic cloves, minced
   2 tablespoons soy sauce

1. Combine garlic, ginger and red pepper flakes in small bowl. Add chicken; toss to coat. Cover; refrigerate 30 minutes, turning occasionally.

2. Remove chicken from marinade; discard marinade. Heat large nonstick skillet over medium-high heat. Add peanuts; cook and stir 2 minutes or until beginning to brown. Remove from skillet; set aside.

3. Heat 1 teaspoon oil in skillet. Add chicken; cook 3 minutes or until cooked through. Remove to plate; set aside.

4. Heat remaining 1 teaspoon oil in skillet; cook onion and carrot 2 minutes. Add broccoli and 1/4 cup broth; bring to a boil over medium-high heat. Cover; cook 2 minutes.

5. Whisk remaining 1 cup broth with cornstarch in small bowl until cornstarch is dissolved. Add cornstarch mixture, chicken and garlic to skillet; cook 1 minute or until sauce is thickened. Remove from heat; sprinkle with soy sauce and peanuts. *Makes 4 servings*

Sweet 'n Sour

1 can (20 ounce) DOLE® Pineapple Chunks
1 pound boneless, skinless chicken breasts
   Salt and black pepper to taste
1 tablespoon vegetable oil
2 DOLE® Carrots, thinly sliced
1 green or red bell pepper, seeded, cut into chunks
1 medium onion, cut into chunks
1 clove garlic, minced
½ cup ketchup
⅓ cup packed brown sugar
1 tablespoon cornstarch
1 tablespoon soy sauce
1 teaspoon ground ginger
   Grated peel and juice from 1 lemon
3 cups hot cooked rice

• Drain pineapple; reserve juice.

• Cut chicken into bite-size pieces. Season with salt and pepper. In large nonstick skillet, brown chicken in oil, in two batches, if necessary. Reduce heat. Add carrots, bell pepper, onion and garlic. Cover; simmer 5 minutes.

• Combine reserved juice, ketchup, brown sugar, cornstarch, soy sauce, ginger, lemon peel and lemon juice. Stir into skillet. Cover, simmer 5 minutes longer. Stir in pineapple until heated through. Serve with rice.

Makes 6 servings

Prep Time: 15 minutes
Cook Time: 15 minutes

Spicy Orange Chicken

¾ **cup all-purpose flour**
½ **teaspoon salt**
¼ **teaspoon baking powder**
1 **pound boneless skinless chicken thighs, cut into 1-inch pieces**
3 **cups vegetable oil**
1 **teaspoon chili oil**
   Grated peel of 2 oranges
4 **whole dried chile peppers**
2 **cloves garlic, minced**
1½ **teaspoons finely chopped fresh ginger**
   Juice of 2 oranges
¼ **cup molasses**
1 **tablespoon soy sauce**
2 **teaspoons cornstarch**
   Hot cooked rice

1. Combine flour, salt and baking powder in medium bowl. Whisk in ¾ cup water to form smooth batter. Add chicken; mix well.

2. Heat about 3 cups vegetable oil in wok over medium-high heat until oil registers 375°F on deep-fry thermometer. Shake off excess batter from one third of chicken; carefully add to wok.

3. Cook about 4 minutes or until chicken is golden brown and cooked through, stirring occasionally to break up pieces with spoon. Remove chicken with slotted spoon to paper towels; drain. Repeat 2 more times with remaining chicken, reheating oil between batches.

4. Drain oil from wok. Reheat wok over medium-high heat; add chili oil. Add orange peel, chile peppers, garlic and ginger; stir-fry about 30 seconds to 1 minute or until fragrant.

5. Combine orange juice, molasses, soy sauce and cornstarch in small bowl; add to wok. Cook and stir until sauce boils and thickens. Return chicken to wok; mix well. Transfer to serving platter; serve with rice.

Makes 4 servings

Kung Po Chicken

1 pound boneless skinless chicken breasts or thighs
2 cloves garlic, minced
1 teaspoon hot chili oil
¼ cup soy sauce
2 teaspoons cornstarch
1 tablespoon peanut or vegetable oil
⅓ cup roasted peanuts
2 green onions, cut into thin strips
Lettuce leaves
Plum sauce

1. Cut chicken into 1-inch pieces. Toss with garlic and chili oil in medium bowl. Blend soy sauce into cornstarch in small bowl until smooth.

2. Heat peanut oil in wok or large skillet over medium-high heat. Add chicken mixture; stir-fry 3 minutes or until chicken is cooked through.

3. Stir cornstarch mixture; add to wok with peanuts and green onions. Cook and stir 1 minute or until sauce boils and thickens.

4. To serve, spread lettuce leaves lightly with plum sauce. Top with chicken mixture.   *Makes 4 servings*

Moo Goo Gai Pan

1 package (1 ounce) dried shiitake mushrooms
¼ cup soy sauce
2 tablespoons rice vinegar
3 cloves garlic, minced
1 pound boneless skinless chicken breasts
½ cup chicken broth
1 tablespoon cornstarch
2 tablespoons peanut or vegetable oil, divided
1 can (about 7 ounces) straw mushrooms, rinsed and drained
3 green onions, cut into 1-inch pieces
Hot cooked Chinese rice noodles or rice (optional)

1. Place dried mushrooms in small bowl; cover with boiling water. Soak 20 minutes to soften. Drain; squeeze out excess water. Discard stems; slice caps.

2. Combine soy sauce, vinegar and garlic in medium bowl. Cut chicken crosswise into ½-inch strips. Add to soy sauce mixture; toss to coat. Marinate 20 minutes at room temperature. Blend broth into cornstarch in small bowl until smooth.

3. Heat oil in wok or large skillet over medium-high heat. Drain chicken, reserving marinade. Add chicken to wok; stir-fry 3 minutes or until cooked through. Remove and set aside. Heat remaining 1 tablespoon oil in wok. Add dried mushrooms, straw mushrooms and green onions; stir-fry 1 minute.

4. Stir cornstarch mixture; add to wok with reserved marinade. Bring to a boil; boil 1 minute or until sauce thickens. Return chicken along with any accumulated juices to wok; cook and stir until heated through. Serve over noodles, if desired. *Makes 4 servings*

Pineapple-Hoisin Hens

1 can (8 ounces) crushed pineapple in juice, undrained
2 tablespoons rice vinegar
2 tablespoons soy sauce
2 tablespoons hoisin sauce
2 teaspoons minced fresh ginger
2 cloves garlic
1 teaspoon Chinese five-spice powder*
2 large Cornish hens (about 1½ pounds each), split in half

Chinese five-spice powder is a blend of cinnamon, cloves, fennel seed, anise and Szechuan peppercorns. It is available in most supermarkets and at Asian grocery stores.

1. Process all ingredients, except hens, in blender or food processor 5 seconds or until fairly smooth.

2. Place hens in large resealable food storage bag; pour pineapple mixture over hens. Seal bag; turn to coat. Marinate in refrigerator at least 2 hours or up to 24 hours, turning bag once.

3. Preheat oven to 375°F. Drain hens; reserve marinade. Place hens, skin side up, on rack in shallow foil-lined roasting pan. Roast 35 minutes.

4. Brush hens lightly with some reserved marinade; discard remaining marinade. Roast 10 minutes or until hens are browned and cooked through (165°F).   *Makes 4 servings*

Twice-Fried Chicken Thighs with Plum Sauce

1 tablespoon sesame seeds
½ cup Plum Sauce (recipe follows)
1 cup peanut oil
1 to 1¼ pounds boneless skinless chicken thighs, cut into strips
4 medium carrots, cut into matchstick-size strips
4 green onions, sliced
½ teaspoon salt
½ teaspoon red pepper flakes
 Hot cooked rice

1. Heat wok over medium-high heat. Add sesame seeds; cook and stir 45 seconds or until golden. Remove to small bowl; set aside.

2. Prepare Plum Sauce.

3. Heat oil in wok over high heat until oil registers 375°F on deep-fry thermometer. Fry chicken 1 minute. Remove with slotted spoon; drain on paper towels. Drain oil from wok, reserving 2 tablespoons.

4. Return 1 tablespoon reserved oil to wok. Heat over high heat. Add carrots; stir-fry 5 minutes until crisp-tender. Remove from wok; set aside.

5. Add remaining 1 tablespoon oil to wok. Add chicken and green onions; stir-fry 1 minute. Stir in Plum Sauce, carrots, salt and red pepper flakes; cook and stir 2 minutes. Serve over rice; sprinkle with sesame seeds.   *Makes 4 servings*

Plum Sauce

1 cup plum preserves
½ cup prepared chutney, chopped
2 tablespoons brown sugar
2 tablespoons lemon juice
2 cloves garlic, minced
2 teaspoons soy sauce
2 teaspoons minced fresh ginger

Combine all ingredients in small saucepan. Cook and stir over medium heat until preserves are melted. *Makes 1 cup*

Sesame Chicken

**1 pound boneless skinless chicken breasts or thighs, cut into
    1-inch pieces**
⅔ cup teriyaki sauce, divided
2 teaspoons cornstarch
1 tablespoon peanut or vegetable oil
2 cloves garlic, minced
2 green onions, cut into ½-inch slices
1 tablespoon sesame seeds, toasted*
1 teaspoon dark sesame oil

**To toast sesame seeds, spread seeds in small skillet. Shake skillet over medium-low heat
3 minutes or until seeds begin to pop and turn golden. Remove from heat.*

1. Toss chicken with ⅓ cup teriyaki sauce in medium bowl. Marinate in refrigerator 15 to 20 minutes.

2. Drain chicken; discard marinade. Blend remaining ⅓ cup teriyaki sauce into cornstarch in small bowl until smooth.

3. Heat peanut oil in wok or large skillet over medium-high heat. Add chicken and garlic; stir-fry 3 minutes or until chicken is cooked through. Stir cornstarch mixture; add to wok. Cook and stir 1 minute or until sauce boils and thickens. Stir in green onions, sesame seeds and sesame oil.

Makes 4 servings

Menu

Easy Seafood Stir-Fry	Five-Spice Shrimp with Walnuts
Garlic Prawns with Green Onion	Szechuan Tuna Steaks
Clams in Black Bean Sauce	Scallop Stir-Fry with Black Bean and Stout Sauce
Red Snapper with Orange-Plum Sauce	Shrimp in Mock Lobster Sauce
Steamed Fish with Broccoli	Stir-Fried Crab
Pan-Cooked Bok Choy Salmon	Lemon Sesame Scallops

Seafood
SPECIALTIES

Pan-Cooked Bok Choy Salmon, page 112

Easy Seafood Stir-Fry

1 package (1 ounce) dried shiitake mushrooms
½ cup chicken broth
2 tablespoons dry sherry
1 tablespoon soy sauce
4½ teaspoons cornstarch
1 teaspoon vegetable oil, divided
½ pound bay scallops or halved sea scallops
¼ pound medium raw shrimp, peeled and deveined
2 cloves garlic, minced
6 ounces (2 cups) fresh snow peas, cut diagonally into halves
2 cups hot cooked rice
¼ cup thinly sliced green onions

1. Place mushrooms in small bowl; cover with boiling water. Soak 20 minutes to soften. Drain; squeeze out excess water. Discard stems; slice caps.

2. Blend broth, sherry and soy sauce into cornstarch in another small bowl until smooth; set aside.

3. Heat ½ teaspoon oil in wok or large nonstick skillet over medium heat. Add scallops, shrimp and garlic; stir-fry 3 minutes or until seafood is opaque. Remove mixture to plate.

4. Add remaining ½ teaspoon oil to wok. Add mushrooms and snow peas; stir-fry 3 minutes or until snow peas are crisp-tender.

5. Stir cornstarch mixture; add to wok. Cook and stir 2 minutes or until sauce boils and thickens. Return seafood and any accumulated juices to wok; cook and stir until heated through. Serve with rice; sprinkle with green onions. *Makes 4 servings*

Garlic Prawns with Green Onion

2 tablespoons cooking oil
1 tablespoon LEE KUM KEE® Minced Garlic
8 ounces prawns, deveined and patted dry
2 tablespoons LEE KUM KEE® Soy Sauce
2 red chili peppers, cut into thin strips
2 green onions, chopped
1 tablespoon LEE KUM KEE® Pure Sesame Oil

1. Heat wok or skillet over high heat until hot. Add cooking oil, LEE KUM KEE Minced Garlic, prawns and LEE KUM KEE Soy Sauce; stir-fry until prawns turn pink.

2. Add chili peppers, green onions and LEE KUM KEE Pure Sesame Oil; cook 1 minute. Transfer to plate and serve immediately.

Makes 2 servings

Prep Time: 15 minutes
Cook Time: 10 minutes

Clams in Black Bean Sauce

24 small hard-shell clams
1½ tablespoons fermented, salted black beans
2 cloves garlic, minced
1 teaspoon minced fresh ginger
2 tablespoons vegetable oil
2 green onions, thinly sliced
1 cup chicken broth
2 tablespoons dry sherry
1 tablespoon soy sauce
1½ to 2 cups Chinese-style thin egg noodles, cooked and drained
3 tablespoons chopped fresh cilantro or parsley

1. Scrub clams under cold running water with stiff brush. (Discard any shells that refuse to close when tapped.)

2. Place black beans in sieve and rinse under cold running water. Coarsely chop beans. Combine beans with garlic and ginger; finely chop together.

3. Heat oil in 5-quart Dutch oven over medium heat. Add black bean mixture and green onions; stir-fry 30 seconds. Add clams and stir to coat.

4. Add chicken broth, sherry and soy sauce to Dutch oven. Bring to a boil. Reduce heat; cover and simmer 5 to 8 minutes until clam shells open. (Discard any clams that do not open.)

5. Arrange clams on noodles. Ladle broth over clams. Garnish with cilantro. *Makes 4 servings*

Red Snapper with Orange-Plum Sauce

1 pound red snapper fillets
2 tablespoons soy sauce
½ cup all-purpose flour
¼ teaspoon salt
⅛ teaspoon black pepper
3 tablespoons plus 1 teaspoon vegetable oil, divided
½ cup orange juice
1 teaspoon cornstarch
1 clove garlic, minced
1 jalapeño pepper, seeded and minced
½ cup plum sauce
2 tablespoons mirin (rice wine)
1 tablespoon chili garlic sauce
1 tablespoon minced green onion (optional)

1. Combine snapper fillets and soy sauce in shallow bowl; turn to coat. Marinate 30 minutes.

2. Combine flour, salt and black pepper on plate. Remove fish from soy sauce; coat with flour mixture.

3. Heat 2 tablespoons oil in large nonstick skillet. Place half of fish in skillet; shake skillet so fish doesn't stick. Cook over medium-high heat 4 to 5 minutes per side. Remove fish from skillet and keep warm. Repeat with remaining 1 tablespoon oil and fish.

4. Stir orange juice into cornstarch in small bowl; mix well. Heat remaining 1 teaspoon oil in small saucepan over medium-high heat. Add garlic and jalapeño; cook and stir 1 minute. Add cornstarch mixture, plum sauce, mirin and chili garlic sauce; cook and stir 1 minute or until slightly thickened.

5. Arrange fish on plates and top with sauce. Garnish with green onion.

Makes 4 servings

Steamed Fish with Broccoli

2 (10- to 12-ounce) halibut steaks (1 inch thick), cut into halves*

3 tablespoons dry white wine

1 tablespoon rice vinegar or white vinegar

½ teaspoon salt, divided

⅛ teaspoon white pepper

1 tablespoon cornstarch

1 tablespoon oyster sauce

1 teaspoon sugar

1 teaspoon dark sesame oil

1 teaspoon soy sauce

3 cups broccoli florets

2 tablespoons vegetable oil, divided

2 teaspoons minced fresh ginger

1 clove garlic, minced

1 pound ripe tomatoes, cut into ½-inch cubes, divided

Lemon wedges (optional)

Or substitute 4 mahi-mahi fillets (about 7 ounces each), folded crosswise in half.

1. Rinse fish and drain on paper towels. Combine wine, vinegar, ¼ teaspoon salt and pepper in large glass bowl; mix well. Add fish; turn to coat. Marinate 30 minutes.

2. Meanwhile, combine cornstarch, oyster sauce, sugar, sesame oil and soy sauce in cup; mix well. Set aside.

3. Place broccoli in medium bowl. Add 1 tablespoon vegetable oil and sprinkle with remaining ¼ teaspoon salt; toss. Set aside.

4. To steam fish, place wire rack in wok. Add water to 1 inch below rack. (Water should not touch rack.) Cover wok; bring water to a boil over high heat. Drain fish and place on heat-proof plate. Arrange broccoli around fish. Place dish on rack. Cover and reduce heat to medium. Steam 8 to 10 minutes or until fish flakes easily when tested with fork. Carefully remove plate from wok; cover and keep warm.

5. Drain water from wok. Heat wok over high heat about 30 seconds or until dry. Drizzle remaining 1 tablespoon vegetable oil into wok; heat 15 seconds. Add ginger and garlic; stir-fry 15 seconds. Add half of tomatoes. Stir-fry 1 minute; reduce heat to low. Cook 2 minutes or until tomatoes soften.

6. Stir cornstarch mixture; add to wok. Cook and stir until sauce boils and thickens. Stir in remaining tomatoes and cook until heated through.

7. Spoon some tomato sauce over fish. Serve with remaining sauce and lemon wedges. *Makes 4 servings*

Pan-Cooked Bok Choy Salmon

1 pound bok choy or napa cabbage, chopped
1 cup broccoli slaw mix
2 tablespoons olive oil, divided
2 salmon fillets (4 to 6 ounces each)
¼ teaspoon salt
½ teaspoon black pepper
1 teaspoon sesame seeds

1. Combine bok choy and broccoli slaw mix in colander; rinse and drain well.

2. Heat 1 tablespoon oil in large nonstick skillet over medium heat. Sprinkle salmon with salt and pepper. Add salmon to skillet; cook about 3 minutes per side. Remove salmon from skillet.

3. Add remaining 1 tablespoon oil and sesame seeds to skillet; stir to toast sesame seeds. Add bok choy mixture; cook and stir 3 to 4 minutes.

4. Return salmon to skillet. Reduce heat to low; cover and cook 4 minutes or until salmon flakes when tested with fork.

Makes 2 servings

Five-Spice Shrimp with Walnuts

1 pound medium raw shrimp, peeled and deveined

2 cloves garlic, minced

½ teaspoon Chinese five-spice powder*

½ cup chicken broth

2 tablespoons soy sauce

2 tablespoons dry sherry

1 tablespoon cornstarch

1 tablespoon peanut or vegetable oil

1 red bell pepper, cut into short, thin strips

⅓ cup walnut halves or quarters

Hot cooked rice (optional)

¼ cup thinly sliced green onions (optional)

*Chinese five-spice powder is a blend of cinnamon, cloves, fennel seed, anise and Szechuan peppercorns. It is available in most supermarkets and at Asian grocery stores.

1. Toss shrimp with garlic and five-spice powder in small bowl.

2. Blend broth, soy sauce and sherry into cornstarch in cup until smooth.

3. Heat oil in wok or large skillet over medium-high heat. Add shrimp mixture, bell pepper and walnuts; stir-fry 3 to 5 minutes until shrimp are opaque and bell pepper is crisp-tender.

4. Stir cornstarch mixture; add to wok. Cook and stir 1 minute or until sauce boils and thickens. Serve over rice, if desired. Garnish with green onions.   *Makes 4 servings*

Szechuan Tuna Steaks

4 tuna steaks (6 ounces each), cut 1 inch thick
¼ cup sake or dry sherry
¼ cup soy sauce
1 tablespoon dark sesame oil
1 teaspoon hot chili oil *or* ¼ teaspoon red pepper flakes
1 clove garlic, minced
3 tablespoons chopped fresh cilantro (optional)

1. Place tuna in single layer in large shallow glass dish. Combine sake, soy sauce, sesame oil, hot chili oil and garlic in small bowl. Reserve ¼ cup soy sauce mixture. Pour remaining soy sauce mixture over tuna. Cover; marinate in refrigerator 40 minutes, turning once.

2. Spray grid with nonstick cooking spray. Prepare grill for direct grilling.

3. Drain tuna, discarding marinade. Grill, uncovered, over medium-hot coals 6 minutes or until tuna is seared but still feels somewhat soft in center,* turning once. Transfer tuna to cutting board. Cut each tuna steak into thin slices; fan out slices onto serving plates. Drizzle tuna slices with reserved soy sauce mixture; sprinkle with cilantro, if desired.

Makes 4 servings

Tuna becomes dry and tough if overcooked. Cook to medium doneness for best results.

Szechuan Tuna Steak

Scallop Stir-Fry with Black Bean and Stout Sauce

1 can (about 15 ounces) black beans, rinsed, drained and chopped
⅓ cup dark-colored beer, such as porter
2 tablespoons soy sauce
2 tablespoons honey
2 teaspoons hoisin sauce
2 cloves garlic, minced
½ teaspoon salt
⅛ teaspoon red pepper flakes
2 tablespoons olive oil
1 medium red bell pepper, seeded and sliced into thin strips
1½ cups fresh snow peas
1½ cups thinly sliced carrots
1½ pounds sea scallops

1. Blend black beans, beer, soy sauce, honey, hoisin sauce, garlic, salt and red pepper flakes in blender or food processor until fairly smooth.

2. Heat oil in large nonstick skillet over medium-high heat. Add bell pepper, snow peas and carrots; cook and stir 3 minutes. Add scallops and black bean sauce; stir-fry 6 to 10 minutes or until scallops are opaque and mixture is heated through. *Makes 4 to 6 servings*

Shrimp in Mock Lobster Sauce

½ **cup beef or chicken broth**
¼ **cup oyster sauce**
 1 **tablespoon cornstarch**
 1 **egg**
 1 **egg white**
 1 **tablespoon peanut or canola oil**
¾ **pound medium or large raw shrimp, peeled and deveined**
 2 **cloves garlic, minced**
 3 **green onions, cut into ½-inch pieces**
 2 **cups hot cooked Chinese egg noodles**

1. Stir broth and oyster sauce into cornstarch in small bowl until smooth; set aside. Beat egg with egg white in separate small bowl.

2. Heat oil in wok over medium-high heat. Add shrimp and garlic; stir-fry 3 to 5 minutes or until shrimp are pink and opaque.

3. Stir broth mixture; add to wok. Add green onions; cook and stir 1 minute or until sauce boils and thickens.

4. Whisk eggs into wok; cook and stir 1 minute or just until eggs are set. Serve over noodles. *Makes 4 servings*

tip

Oyster sauce is a rich-tasting, dark brown sauce made from oysters and soy sauce. Check the label to see if the sauce you're purchasing contains real oyster extract or just oyster flavoring. After opening, store oyster sauce in the refrigerator.

Shrimp in Mock Lobster Sauce

Stir-Fried Crab

8 ounces firm tofu, drained
1 tablespoon soy sauce
¼ cup chicken broth
3 tablespoons oyster sauce
2 teaspoons cornstarch
1 tablespoon peanut or vegetable oil
2 cups snow peas, cut into halves
8 ounces thawed frozen cooked crabmeat or imitation crabmeat, broken into ½-inch pieces (about 2 cups)
  Sesame Noodle Cake (recipe follows)
2 tablespoons chopped fresh cilantro or thinly sliced green onion

1. Press tofu lightly between paper towels; cut into ½-inch squares or triangles. Place in shallow dish. Drizzle soy sauce over tofu.

2. Blend broth and oyster sauce into cornstarch in small bowl until smooth.

3. Heat oil in wok or large skillet over medium-high heat. Add snow peas; stir-fry 2 minutes or until crisp-tender. Add crabmeat; stir-fry 1 minute. Stir cornstarch mixture; add to wok. Cook and stir 30 seconds or until sauce boils and thickens.

4. Stir in tofu mixture; cook and stir until heated through. Serve over Sesame Noodle Cake. Sprinkle with cilantro.   *Makes 4 servings*

Sesame Noodle Cake

4 ounces uncooked thin Chinese egg noodles or vermicelli
1 tablespoon soy sauce
1 tablespoon peanut or vegetable oil
½ teaspoon dark sesame oil

1. Cook noodles according to package directions; drain well. Place in large bowl. Toss with soy sauce.

2. Heat peanut oil in large nonstick skillet over medium heat. Add noodle mixture; pat into even layer with spatula.

3. Cook 6 minutes or until bottom is lightly browned. Invert onto plate, then slide back into skillet, browned side up. Cook 4 minutes or until bottom is browned. Drizzle with sesame oil. Transfer to serving platter and cut into quarters.

Makes 4 servings

Lemon Sesame Scallops

8 ounces uncooked whole wheat spaghetti, cooked and drained
3 tablespoons sesame oil, divided
¼ cup chicken broth or clam juice
½ teaspoon grated lemon peel
3 tablespoons lemon juice
2 tablespoons oyster sauce
1 tablespoon cornstarch
1 tablespoon soy sauce
1 tablespoon vegetable oil
2 carrots, cut into matchstick-size strips
1 yellow bell pepper, cut into thin strips
1 teaspoon minced fresh ginger
1 clove garlic, minced
1 pound sea scallops
6 ounces fresh snow peas, trimmed
2 green onions, thinly sliced
1 tablespoon sesame seeds, toasted

1. Toss spaghetti with 2 tablespoons sesame oil. Cover; keep warm. Blend broth, lemon peel, lemon juice, oyster sauce, cornstarch and soy sauce in small bowl until smooth; set aside. Heat remaining 1 tablespoon sesame oil and vegetable oil in wok or large skillet over medium heat. Add carrots and bell pepper; stir-fry 4 to 5 minutes or until crisp-tender. Transfer to large bowl.

2. Add ginger and garlic to skillet; stir-fry 1 minute over medium-high heat. Add scallops, snow peas and green onions; stir-fry 2 to 3 minutes. Transfer to bowl with vegetable mixture, leaving any liquid in skillet.

3. Add cornstarch mixture to skillet; cook and stir 5 minutes or until thickened. Return scallop mixture to skillet; cook 1 minute or until heated through. Serve immediately over warm spaghetti; sprinkle with sesame seeds.   *Makes 4 servings*

Menu

Stir-Fried Eggplant and Tofu

Green Beans and Shiitake Mushrooms

Chinese Spinach Toss

Mu Shu Vegetables

Chinese Sweet and Sour Vegetables

Fried Tofu with Asian Vegetables

Roasted Shanghai Pepper Salad

Spinach and Mushroom Stir-Fry

Spicy Oriental Green Beans

Carrots Chinoise

Mongolian Vegetables

Treasured
VEGETABLES

Chinese Sweet and Sour Vegetables, page 134

Stir-Fried Eggplant and Tofu

1 green onion
4 ounces lean ground pork
2 cloves garlic, minced
1 teaspoon minced fresh ginger
½ teaspoon dark sesame oil
4 ounces firm tofu
½ cup chicken broth
½ teaspoon cornstarch
1 pound Asian eggplants
2 tablespoons peanut oil
1 tablespoon soy sauce
1 teaspoon Chinese chili garlic sauce
½ teaspoon sugar

1. Mince white part of green onion. Cut green part of onion diagonally into 1½-inch lengths; reserve for garnish.

2. Combine pork, minced green onion, garlic, ginger and sesame oil in small bowl.

3. Drain tofu on paper towels. Cut into ½-inch cubes.

4. Stir chicken broth into cornstarch in small bowl; set aside.

5. Cut eggplants lengthwise into quarters, then into 1-inch-thick pieces.

6. Heat peanut oil in wok or large skillet over high heat. Add eggplants; stir-fry 5 to 6 minutes or until tender. Add tofu; stir-fry 1 minute. Remove eggplant and tofu from wok; set aside.

7. Add pork mixture to wok; stir fry about 2 minutes or until brown. Add soy sauce, chili sauce and sugar; cook and stir until heated through.

8. Return eggplant and tofu to wok. Stir cornstarch mixture; add to wok. Cook and stir until sauce thickens. *Makes 4 servings*

Stir-Fried Eggplant and Tofu

Green Beans and Shiitake Mushrooms

10 to 12 dried shiitake mushrooms
¾ cup water, divided
3 tablespoons oyster sauce
1 tablespoon cornstarch
4 cloves garlic, minced
⅛ teaspoon red pepper flakes
1 tablespoon vegetable oil
1 pound fresh green beans, ends trimmed
⅓ cup slivered fresh basil or chopped fresh cilantro
2 green onions, sliced diagonally
⅓ cup roasted peanuts

1. Place mushrooms in bowl; cover with hot water. Let stand 30 minutes or until caps are soft. Drain mushrooms; squeeze out excess water. Remove and discard stems. Slice caps into thin strips.

2. Combine ¼ cup water, oyster sauce, cornstarch, garlic and red pepper flakes in small bowl; mix well. Set aside.

3. Heat oil in wok or medium skillet over medium-high heat. Add mushrooms, beans and remaining ½ cup water; cook and stir until water boils. Reduce heat to medium-low; cover and cook 8 to 10 minutes or until beans are crisp-tender, stirring occasionally.

4. Stir cornstarch mixture; add to wok. Cook and stir until sauce thickens and coats beans. (If cooking water has evaporated, add enough water to form thick sauce.) Add basil, green onions and peanuts; mix well. Transfer to serving platter.   *Makes 4 to 6 servings*

Chinese Spinach Toss

**3 to 4 cups fresh bean sprouts *or* 2 cans (16 ounces each) bean
    sprouts, well drained**

⅓ cup honey

⅓ cup white wine or rice vinegar

2 tablespoons vegetable oil

2 teaspoons soy sauce

1 to 2 teaspoons grated fresh ginger

6 cups washed and torn fresh spinach

1 cup diced peeled jicama

1 cup crisp Chinese noodles

Place bean sprouts in large glass or ceramic bowl. Combine honey,
vinegar, oil, soy sauce and ginger in small bowl; pour over bean sprouts.
Cover and refrigerate at least 1 hour, tossing occasionally. Just before
serving, add spinach and jicama; toss gently to coat. Top each serving
with noodles. *Makes 6 servings*

Favorite recipe from **National Honey Board**

Mu Shu Vegetables

Peanut Sauce (recipe follows)
3 tablespoons soy sauce
2 tablespoons dry sherry
1½ tablespoons minced fresh ginger
2 teaspoons cornstarch
3 cloves garlic, minced
1½ teaspoons sesame oil
1 tablespoon peanut oil
3 leeks, washed and cut into 2-inch slivers
3 carrots, cut into matchstick-size strips
1 cup thinly sliced fresh shiitake mushrooms
1 small head Napa or Savoy cabbage, shredded (about 4 cups)
2 cups bean sprouts, rinsed and drained
8 ounces firm tofu, drained and cut into 2½×¼-inch strips
12 (8-inch) flour tortillas, warmed*
¾ cup finely chopped honey roasted peanuts

*Stack tortillas and wrap in plastic wrap. Microwave on HIGH 30 seconds to 1 minute.

1. Prepare Peanut Sauce; set aside. Whisk soy sauce, sherry, ginger, cornstarch, garlic and sesame oil in small bowl until smooth; set aside.

2. Heat peanut oil in wok over medium-high heat 1 minute. Add leeks, carrots and mushrooms; stir-fry 2 minutes. Add cabbage; stir-fry 3 minutes or until just tender. Add bean sprouts and tofu; stir-fry 1 minute. Stir soy sauce mixture; add to wok. Cook and stir 1 minute or until sauce is thickened.

3. Spread each tortilla with about 1 teaspoon Peanut Sauce. Spoon ½ cup vegetable mixture onto bottom half of each tortilla; sprinkle with 1 tablespoon peanuts. Fold bottom edge of tortilla over filling; fold in side edges. Roll up to completely enclose filling. Serve with Peanut Sauce.

Makes 6 servings

Peanut Sauce

3 tablespoons sugar
3 tablespoons water
3 tablespoons dry sherry
3 tablespoons soy sauce
2 teaspoons white wine vinegar
⅓ cup creamy peanut butter

Combine all ingredients except peanut butter in small saucepan. Bring to a boil over medium-high heat, stirring constantly. Boil 1 minute or until sugar melts. Stir in peanut butter until smooth; cool to room temperature.

Makes ⅔ cup

Chinese Sweet and Sour Vegetables

3 cups broccoli florets

2 medium carrots, diagonally sliced

1 large red bell pepper, cut into thin strips

¼ cup water

2 teaspoons cornstarch

1 teaspoon sugar

⅓ cup unsweetened pineapple juice

1 tablespoon rice vinegar

1 tablespoon soy sauce

½ teaspoon dark sesame oil

¼ cup chopped fresh cilantro (optional)

1. Combine broccoli, carrots and bell pepper in large skillet. Add water; bring to a boil over high heat. Reduce heat to medium. Cover; steam 4 minutes or until vegetables are crisp-tender. Drain vegetables.

2. Combine cornstarch and sugar in small bowl. Blend in pineapple juice, vinegar and soy sauce until smooth.

3. Stir cornstarch mixture; add to skillet. Cook and stir 2 minutes or until sauce boils and thickens. Return vegetables to skillet; toss with sauce. Stir in sesame oil. Garnish with cilantro. *Makes 4 servings*

Fried Tofu with Asian Vegetables

1 pound firm tofu, drained, cut into ¾-inch cubes

½ cup soy sauce, divided

1 cup all-purpose flour

¾ teaspoon salt, divided

⅛ teaspoon black pepper

**   Vegetable oil for frying**

2 packages (16 ounces each) frozen mixed Asian vegetables*

3 tablespoons water

1 teaspoon cornstarch

3 tablespoons plum sauce

2 tablespoons lemon juice

2 teaspoons sugar

1 teaspoon minced fresh ginger

⅛ to ¼ teaspoon red pepper flakes

*Frozen vegetables do not need to be thawed before cooking.

1. Gently mix tofu and ¼ cup soy sauce in shallow bowl; let stand 5 minutes. Combine flour, ½ teaspoon salt and black pepper on plate. Gently toss tofu cubes with flour mixture to coat.

2. Heat 1½ inches oil in Dutch oven. Test heat by dropping 1 tofu cube into oil; it should brown in 1 minute. Fry tofu cubes in small batches until browned. Remove from oil with slotted spoon; drain on paper towels.

3. Drain all but 1 tablespoon oil from Dutch oven. Add vegetables and remaining ¼ teaspoon salt. Cook and stir over medium-high heat about 6 minutes or until vegetables are heated through. Increase heat to high to evaporate any remaining liquid. Set aside and cover to keep warm.

4. Stir water into cornstarch in small bowl until well blended. Combine cornstarch mixture, remaining ¼ cup soy sauce, plum sauce, lemon juice, sugar, ginger and red pepper flakes in small saucepan; cook and stir over low heat 1 to 2 minutes or until sauce is slightly thickened. Top with tofu and sauce; toss gently to mix.   *Makes 6 servings*

Roasted Shanghai Pepper Salad

1 jar (about 15 ounces) roasted red or yellow peppers
1½ tablespoons soy sauce
1 tablespoon rice vinegar
1 tablespoon dark sesame oil
2 teaspoons honey
1 clove garlic, minced
Romaine lettuce or spinach leaves
2 tablespoons coarsely chopped fresh cilantro

1. Drain and rinse peppers; pat dry with paper towels. Cut peppers lengthwise into ½-inch strips; place in small bowl.

2. Combine soy sauce, vinegar, sesame oil, honey and garlic; mix well. Pour over peppers; cover and refrigerate at least 2 hours. Serve over lettuce leaves. Sprinkle with cilantro. *Makes 4 servings*

Note: This salad will keep up to 1 week if covered and refrigerated.

tip

Roasted peppers in the jar are marinated in garlic, salt and vinegar. They make a perfect addition to any Chinese flavored salad.

Spinach and Mushroom Stir-Fry

2 tablespoons peanut oil
2 cloves garlic, minced
1 teaspoon minced fresh ginger
¼ to ½ teaspoon red pepper flakes
1 red bell pepper, cut into 1-inch pieces
2 ounces shiitake or button mushrooms,* sliced
10 ounces spinach, stemmed and coarsely chopped
1 teaspoon fish sauce

Or substitute ½ ounce dried shiitake mushrooms, soaked according to package directions.

1. Heat oil in wok over high heat 1 minute. Add garlic, ginger and red pepper flakes; stir-fry 30 seconds.

2. Add bell pepper and mushrooms; stir-fry 2 minutes. Add spinach and fish sauce; stir-fry 1 to 2 minutes or until spinach is wilted.

Makes 4 servings

Spicy Oriental Green Beans

1 pound whole green beans, trimmed
2 tablespoons chopped green onions
2 tablespoons dry sherry or chicken broth
4½ teaspoons soy sauce
1 teaspoon chili sauce with garlic
1 teaspoon dark sesame oil
1 clove garlic, minced

1. Fill Dutch oven with water to depth of ½ inch; bring to a boil. Place green beans in steamer basket in Dutch oven. Cover; steam about 5 minutes or until crisp-tender. Drain and set aside.

2. Combine green onions, sherry, soy sauce, chili sauce, sesame oil and garlic in small bowl. Spray Dutch oven with nonstick cooking spray; heat over medium heat. Add green beans; pour soy sauce mixture over beans. Toss well to coat. Cook and stir 3 to 5 minutes until heated through.

Makes 4 servings

Carrots Chinoise

8 ounces medium carrots, cut diagonally into thin slices
2 teaspoons vegetable oil
¼ cup water
1 can (8 ounces) sliced water chestnuts, drained
1 package (6 ounces) frozen Chinese pea pods, partially thawed
1 teaspoon dark sesame oil
½ teaspoon salt
⅛ teaspoon black pepper
   Black sesame seeds (optional)

1. Heat vegetable oil in wok over medium-high heat 1 minute. Add carrots; stir-fry until lightly browned. Reduce heat to medium.

2. Add water; cover and cook about 4 minutes or until carrots are crisp-tender.

3. Add water chestnuts, pea pods, sesame oil, salt and black pepper; stir-fry until heated through. Sprinkle with sesame seeds.

Makes 4 servings

tip

Water chestnuts are the edible fruit of an aquatic plant native to Southeast Asia. Fresh water chestnuts can usually be found in Asian markets, but the bulk of the American supply comes canned whole or sliced. Typically used as an ingredient in stir-fries, water chestnuts are also added to salads, pilafs and entrées for their crunchiness.

Mongolian Vegetables

1 package (about 14 ounces) firm tofu
4 tablespoons soy sauce, divided
1 tablespoon dark sesame oil
1 large head bok choy (about 1½ pounds)
2 teaspoons cornstarch
1 tablespoon peanut or vegetable oil
1 red or yellow bell pepper, cut into short thin strips
2 cloves garlic, minced
4 green onions, cut into ½-inch pieces
2 teaspoons sesame seeds, toasted*

*To toast sesame seeds, spread seeds in small skillet. Shake skillet over medium-low heat 3 minutes or until seeds begin to pop and turn golden. Remove from heat.

1. Press tofu lightly between paper towels to drain excess water; cut into ¾-inch squares. Place in shallow dish. Combine 2 tablespoons soy sauce and sesame oil in small bowl; drizzle over tofu.

2. Cut stems from bok choy leaves; slice stems into ½-inch pieces. Cut leaves crosswise into ½-inch slices.

3. Blend remaining 2 tablespoons soy sauce into cornstarch in small bowl until smooth.

4. Heat peanut oil in wok or large skillet over medium-high heat. Add bok choy stems, bell pepper and garlic; stir-fry 5 minutes. Add bok choy leaves and green onions; stir-fry 2 minutes.

5. Stir cornstarch mixture; add to wok along with tofu mixture. Stir-fry 30 seconds or until sauce boils and thickens. Sprinkle with sesame seeds.

Makes 2 main-dish or 4 side-dish servings

Menu

Luscious Lo Mein

Shrimp Fried Rice

Chicken Fried Rice

Orange-Ginger Tofu & Noodles

Easy Fried Rice

Hong Kong Fried Rice Cakes

Ginger Noodles with Sesame Egg Strips

Three-Topped Rice

Bean Threads with Minced Pork

Sizzling Rice Cakes with
Mushrooms and Bell Peppers

Noodles with Baby Shrimp

Rice & NOODLES

Three-Topped Rice, page 156

Luscious Lo Mein

8 ounces uncooked lo mein or udon noodles or spaghetti

2 tablespoons vegetable oil

1 package JENNIE-O TURKEY STORE® Boneless Breast Tenderloins,
   cut into ¾-inch chunks

2 teaspoons bottled or fresh minced ginger

2 teaspoons bottled or fresh minced garlic

¼ teaspoon crushed red pepper flakes

2 cups sliced bok choy or fresh sugar snap peas

1 cup thin red bell pepper strips

¼ cup chicken broth

¼ cup soy sauce or tamari

2 tablespoons oyster sauce

2 tablespoons dark sesame oil

Cook noodles according to package directions. Meanwhile, heat
1 tablespoon vegetable oil in large deep skillet over medium-high heat.
Add turkey, ginger, garlic and pepper flakes; stir-fry 3 minutes. Transfer
to bowl; set aside. Add remaining 1 tablespoon vegetable oil to skillet.
Add bok choy and bell pepper; stir-fry 2 minutes. Add broth, soy sauce
and oyster sauce; bring to a simmer. Add turkey and sesame oil to skillet;
simmer 2 minutes or until turkey is no longer pink in center. Drain
noodles; add to skillet and heat through. Serve in shallow soup bowls.

Makes 6 servings

Prep Time: 30 minutes
Cook Time: 15 minutes

Shrimp Fried Rice

- 1 teaspoon vegetable oil
- 1 pound medium shrimp, peeled and deveined
- ½ cup red bell pepper, diced
- 2 cups snow peas, sliced diagonally
- 2 cups cooked SUCCESS®, MAHATMA®, CAROLINA® or RICELAND® Whole Grain Brown Rice
- ¼ cup prepared bottled stir-fry sauce

Heat oil in a large wok or skillet over high heat. Add shrimp and stir-fry 3 minutes. Add bell pepper and snow peas; continue cooking 2 minutes. Add rice and stir-fry sauce; stir 1 more minute or until sauce coats all ingredients and is heated through.   *Makes 4 servings*

Chicken Fried Rice

- 2 Tyson® Trimmed & Ready™ Fresh Boneless Skinless Chicken Breasts
- 2 teaspoons vegetable oil
- ½ cup sliced green onion
- ¼ cup chopped red bell pepper
- 1 clove garlic, crushed
- ½ teaspoon ground ginger
- 3 cups long-grain rice, cooked and chilled
- 2 tablespoons reduced-sodium soy sauce
- ½ cup egg substitute

1. Wash hands. Cut chicken into ½-inch strips. Wash hands.

2. Heat oil in large nonstick skillet or wok over medium-high heat. Cook and stir chicken 3 to 4 minutes or until internal juices of chicken run clear. (Or insert instant-read meat thermometer into thickest part of chicken. Temperature should read 180°F.) Remove chicken from skillet.

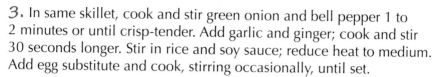

3. In same skillet, cook and stir green onion and bell pepper 1 to 2 minutes or until crisp-tender. Add garlic and ginger; cook and stir 30 seconds longer. Stir in rice and soy sauce; reduce heat to medium. Add egg substitute and cook, stirring occasionally, until set.

4. Return chicken to skillet and cook just until heated through. Refrigerate leftovers immediately.   *Makes 4 servings*

Serving Suggestion: Serve with fresh steamed asparagus.

Prep Time: 15 minutes
Cook Time: 8 minutes
Total Time: 23 minutes

Orange-Ginger Tofu & Noodles

⅔ **cup orange juice**

3 **tablespoons soy sauce**

1 **clove garlic, minced**

½ **to 1 teaspoon minced fresh ginger**

¼ **teaspoon red pepper flakes**

5 **ounces extra-firm tofu, well drained* and cut into ½-inch cubes**

1½ **teaspoons cornstarch**

1 **teaspoon canola or peanut oil**

2 **cups fresh cut-up vegetables such as broccoli, carrots, onion and snow peas**

1½ **cups hot cooked vermicelli**

*Remove any remaining water by placing the block of tofu on several layers of paper towels and covering it with additional paper towels weighted down with a heavy plate. Let it stand for 15 to 20 minutes before cutting into cubes.

1. Combine orange juice, soy sauce, garlic, ginger and red pepper flakes in resealable food storage bag; add tofu. Marinate 20 to 30 minutes. Drain tofu, reserving marinade. Stir marinade into cornstarch in small bowl until smooth.

2. Heat oil in wok or large nonstick skillet over medium-high heat. Add vegetables; stir-fry 2 to 3 minutes or until vegetables are crisp-tender. Add tofu; stir-fry 1 minute. Stir cornstarch mixture; add to skillet. Bring to a boil; boil 1 minute. Serve over noodles.   *Makes 2 servings*

Easy Fried Rice

¼ cup BERTOLLI® Olive Oil
4 cups cooked rice
2 cloves garlic, finely chopped
1 envelope LIPTON® RECIPE SECRETS® Onion Mushroom Soup Mix
½ cup water
1 tablespoon soy sauce
1 cup frozen peas and carrots, partially thawed
2 eggs, lightly beaten

1. In 12-inch nonstick skillet, heat olive oil over medium-high heat and cook rice, stirring constantly, 2 minutes or until rice is heated through. Stir in garlic.

2. Stir in soup mix blended with water and soy sauce and cook 1 minute. Stir in peas and carrots and cook 2 minutes or until heated through.

3. Make a well in center of rice and quickly stir in eggs until cooked.

Makes 4 servings

Prep Time: 10 minutes
Cook Time: 10 minutes

Hong Kong Fried Rice Cakes

1 package (about 6 ounces) chicken-flavored rice and vermicelli mix
½ cup sliced green onions
2 eggs, beaten
2 tablespoons chopped fresh parsley
1 tablespoon hoisin sauce
1 tablespoon soy sauce
1 teaspoon minced fresh ginger
1 clove garlic, minced
2 to 3 tablespoons vegetable oil, divided

1. Prepare rice according to package directions, omitting butter. Cover and refrigerate one hour or until completely chilled. Add remaining ingredients except oil; mix well. Form rice mixture into cakes, 3 inches in diameter.

2. Heat 1 tablespoon oil in large skillet over medium heat. Cook cakes, in batches, 4 minutes on each side or until golden brown. Add additional oil to skillet as needed. *Makes 4 to 6 servings*

Ginger Noodles with Sesame Egg Strips

5 egg whites
6 teaspoons teriyaki sauce, divided
3 teaspoons toasted sesame seeds,* divided
1 teaspoon dark sesame oil
½ cup chicken broth
1 tablespoon minced fresh ginger
6 ounces Chinese rice noodles or vermicelli, cooked and well
    drained
⅓ cup sliced green onions

*To toast sesame seeds, spread seeds in small skillet. Shake skillet over medium heat 2 minutes or until seeds begin to pop and turn golden. Remove from heat.

1. Beat egg whites, 2 teaspoons teriyaki sauce and 1 teaspoon sesame seeds in large bowl.

2. Heat oil in large nonstick skillet over medium heat. Pour egg mixture into skillet; cook 1½ to 2 minutes or until bottom of omelet is set. Turn omelet over; cook 30 seconds to 1 minute. Slide out onto plate; cool and cut into ½-inch strips.

3. Add broth, ginger and remaining 4 teaspoons teriyaki sauce to skillet. Bring to a boil over high heat; reduce heat to medium. Add noodles; heat through. Add omelet strips and green onions; heat through. Sprinkle with remaining 2 teaspoons sesame seeds. *Makes 4 servings*

Three-Topped Rice

1 ounce Pickled Ginger Slices (recipe follows, optional)
2½ cups short-grain rice
4¼ cups water, divided
1 teaspoon salt, divided
1½ cups fresh or frozen green peas
1 piece fresh ginger (about 1-inch square), grated
2 tablespoons sugar, divided
2 tablespoons sake or dry sherry, divided
1 tablespoon plus 1 teaspoon soy sauce, divided
8 ounces ground chicken
4 eggs, lightly beaten

1. Prepare Pickled Ginger Slices, if desired. Place rice in large bowl; add cold water to cover. Stir rice gently with fingers. (Water will become cloudy.) Drain rice in colander. Repeat washing and draining 3 or 4 times until water remains almost clear. Place rice in large, heavy saucepan. Add 2¾ cups water; soak 30 minutes. Gently stir ½ teaspoon salt into rice. Cover; bring to a boil over medium-high heat. Reduce heat to low; simmer about 15 minutes or until liquid is absorbed. *Do not lift lid during cooking.* Remove pan from heat; let stand, covered, 15 minutes. Gently fluff rice with wooden spoon. Lay dry kitchen towel over saucepan; cover with lid. Let stand 10 minutes to absorb excess moisture.

2. Cut Pickled Ginger Slices into thin strips; set aside. Place peas, remaining 1½ cups water and ½ teaspoon salt in small saucepan. Bring to a boil over medium-high heat; boil 4 minutes or until peas are tender. Drain well. Squeeze grated ginger between thumb and fingers to extract juice into cup. Squeeze enough ginger to measure 1 teaspoon ginger juice. Combine 1 tablespoon sugar, 1 tablespoon sake, 1 tablespoon soy sauce and ginger juice in medium saucepan; bring to a boil over high heat. Add chicken; cook and stir 3 to 4 minutes or until chicken is no longer pink. Turn off heat.

3. Place eggs, remaining 1 tablespoon sugar, 1 tablespoon sake and 1 teaspoon soy sauce in medium skillet. Cook and stir 3 to 5 minutes over medium-low heat until eggs are set but still moist. Remove from heat.

4. Divide rice among four individual serving bowls. Place equal amounts of chicken, peas and eggs over rice. Garnish with Pickled Ginger Slices.

Makes 4 servings

Pickled Ginger Slices

4 ounces fresh ginger, peeled
1 cup boiling water
½ cup rice vinegar
2 tablespoons sugar
½ teaspoon salt

Cut ginger crosswise into thin slices. Place in small bowl; add boiling water. Let stand 30 seconds; drain well. Place vinegar, sugar and salt in small glass or ceramic bowl; stir until sugar is dissolved. Add ginger; stir to coat well. Cover bowl; let stand at room temperature at least 1 hour. Refrigerate, covered, until well chilled.

Makes about ¾ cup

Bean Threads with Minced Pork

4 ounces bean threads or Chinese rice vermicelli

3 dried mushrooms

1 small red or green hot chile pepper, seeded and minced*

3 green onions, divided

2 tablespoons minced fresh ginger

2 tablespoons hot black bean sauce

1½ cups chicken broth

1 tablespoon soy sauce

1 tablespoon dry sherry

2 tablespoons vegetable oil

6 ounces ground pork

2 cilantro sprigs (optional)

*Chile peppers can sting and irritate the skin; wear rubber gloves when handling peppers and do not touch your eyes. Wash hands after handling.

1. Place bean threads and dried mushrooms in separate bowls. Cover each with hot water. Let stand 30 minutes; drain. Cut bean threads into 4-inch pieces. Squeeze out excess water from mushrooms. Cut off and discard stems; cut caps into thin slices.

2. Thinly slice 2 green onions. Cut remaining green onion into 1½-inch slivers; reserve for garnish. Combine ginger and black bean sauce in small bowl. Combine chicken broth, soy sauce and sherry in medium bowl.

3. Heat oil in wok or large skillet over high heat. Add pork; stir-fry about 2 minutes or until no longer pink. Add chile pepper, sliced green onions and ginger-bean sauce mixture. Stir-fry until meat absorbs color from bean sauce, about 1 minute.

4. Add chicken broth mixture, bean threads and mushrooms. Simmer, uncovered, about 5 minutes or until most liquid is absorbed. Garnish with reserved green onion slivers and cilantro sprigs.

Makes 4 servings

Sizzling Rice Cakes with Mushrooms and Bell Peppers

 ¾ **cup short grain rice***
1¾ **cups water, divided**
 1 **can (about 14 ounces) chicken broth**
 1 **tablespoon soy sauce**
 2 **teaspoons sugar**
 2 **teaspoons red wine vinegar**
 2 **tablespoons cornstarch**
 3 **tablespoons peanut oil, divided**
1½ **teaspoons finely chopped fresh ginger**
 2 **cloves garlic, thinly sliced**
 1 **red bell pepper, cut into strips**
 1 **green bell pepper, cut into strips**
 8 **ounces button mushrooms, quartered**
 4 **ounces fresh shiitake or other exotic mushrooms, sliced**
 1 **teaspoon sesame oil**
   Vegetable oil for frying

Short grain rice is preferred for this recipe because of it's high starch content and sticky texture when cooked. It also may be referred to as pearl or glutinous rice. Look for it in most large supermarkets.

1. Rinse rice under cold running water to remove excess starch. Combine rice and 1½ cups water in medium saucepan. Bring to a boil over medium-high heat. Reduce heat to low; cover and simmer 15 to 20 minutes until liquid is absorbed. Cool.

2. Combine broth, soy sauce, sugar and vinegar in medium bowl. Combine cornstarch and remaining ¼ cup water in small cup; mix well. Set aside.

3. Heat 1 tablespoon peanut oil in wok over medium-high heat. Add ginger and garlic; stir-fry 10 seconds. Add pepper strips; stir-fry 2 to 3 minutes or until crisp-tender. Remove and set aside.

4. Add remaining 2 tablespoons peanut oil to wok. Add mushrooms; stir-fry 2 to 3 minutes or until softened. Remove and set aside.

5. Add broth mixture to wok and bring to a boil. Stir cornstarch mixture; add to wok. Cook and stir until sauce boils and thickens slightly. Stir in sesame oil; return vegetables to wok. Remove from heat; cover to keep warm.

6. Shape rice into 12 (2-inch) cakes. (Wet hands to make handling rice easier.)

7. Heat 2 inches vegetable oil in large skillet over medium-high heat until oil registers 375°F on deep-fry thermometer. Add 4 rice cakes; cook 2 to 3 minutes or until puffed and golden, turning once. Remove with slotted spatula to paper towels. Repeat with remaining rice cakes, reheating oil between batches.

8. Place rice cakes in serving bowl. Stir vegetable mixture; pour over rice cakes. *Makes 4 to 6 servings*

Noodles with Baby Shrimp

1 package (3¾ ounces) bean thread noodles

3 green onions, cut into 1-inch pieces

1 tablespoon vegetable oil

1 package (16 ounces) frozen mixed vegetables such as cauliflower, broccoli and carrots

1 cup vegetable broth

8 ounces frozen baby shrimp, thawed

1 tablespoon soy sauce

2 teaspoons dark sesame oil

¼ teaspoon black pepper

1. Place noodles in large bowl. Cover with boiling water; let stand 10 minutes or until softened. Drain noodles. Cut noodles into 5-inch pieces; set aside.

2. Heat vegetable oil in wok over high heat about 1 minute. Add green onions; stir-fry 1 minute. Add mixed vegetables; stir-fry 2 minutes. Add broth; bring to a boil. Reduce heat to low; cover and cook 5 minutes or until vegetables are crisp-tender.

3. Add shrimp to wok; cook until heated through. Stir in noodles, soy sauce, sesame oil and pepper; stir-fry until heated through.

Makes 4 to 6 servings

Menu

Sesame Ginger-Glazed
Tofu with Rice

Mandarin Chicken Salad

Mu Shu Meatball Wraps

Hoisin-Orange Chicken
Wraps

Asian Grilled Steak

Fortune Cookies

Sesame Hoisin
Beer-Can Chicken

Asian Glazed Short Ribs

Golden Gate Chinese
Chicken and Cabbage
Sesame Salad

Oriental Salad Supreme

Green Tea Lychee Frappé

Sesame Chicken Slaw

Chinese Almond Cookies

Szechuan Chicken Tenders

East Meets WEST

Oriental Salad Supreme, page 179

Sesame Ginger-Glazed Tofu with Rice

1 package (14 ounces) extra-firm tofu
1 cup sesame ginger stir-fry sauce, divided
1 cup uncooked long grain rice
4 medium carrots, chopped (about 1 cup)
4 ounces snow peas, halved (about 1 cup)

1. Slice tofu in half crosswise. Cut each half into 2 triangles. Place tofu triangles on cutting board between layers of paper towels. Place another cutting board on top to press moisture out of tofu. Let stand about 15 minutes.

2. Spread ½ cup stir-fry sauce over bottom of baking dish. Place tofu in sauce; marinate at room temperature 30 minutes, turning after 15 minutes.

3. Meanwhile, cook rice according to package directions. Keep warm.

4. Spray indoor grill pan with nonstick cooking spray; heat over medium-high heat. Grill tofu 6 to 8 minutes or until lightly browned, turning after 4 minutes.

5. Meanwhile, pour remaining ½ cup stir-fry sauce into large nonstick skillet; heat over medium-high heat. Add carrots and snow peas; cook and stir 4 to 6 minutes or until crisp-tender. Add rice; stir to combine.

6. Divide rice mixture between 4 plates; top each with tofu triangle.

Makes 4 servings

Mandarin Chicken Salad

2 bags (6 ounces each) Tyson® Refrigerated Fully Cooked Grilled
    Chicken Breast Strips

½ cup bottled sesame-ginger salad dressing

1 can (8 ounces) water chestnuts, drained and chopped
    (about 1 cup)

1 package (6 ounces) frozen pea pods, thawed

6 green onions, thinly sliced (about ½ cup)

½ red bell pepper, seeded and thinly sliced

4 cups torn romaine lettuce

1 can (11 ounces) mandarin oranges, drained

2 cups Chinese chow mein noodles

1. Combine chicken and salad dressing, stirring to coat. Cover and refrigerate 1 hour to marinate.

2. Add water chestnuts, pea pods, green onions, bell pepper and lettuce to chicken mixture. Toss to mix well. Stir in mandarin oranges. Serve salad over chow mein noodles. Refrigerate leftovers immediately.

Makes 4 servings

Prep Time: 15 minutes

Mandarin Chicken Salad

East Meets WEST

Mu Shu Meatball Wraps

Meatballs

> 1 pound lean ground turkey or lean ground beef
>
> ¾ cup QUAKER® Oats (quick or old fashioned, uncooked)
>
> ½ cup finely chopped water chestnuts
>
> ⅓ cup chopped green onions
>
> 1 clove garlic, minced
>
> 1 teaspoon finely chopped fresh ginger or ¼ teaspoon ground ginger
>
> ¼ cup light soy sauce
>
> 1 tablespoon water

Wraps

> ¾ cup prepared plum sauce
>
> 6 (10-inch) flour tortillas, warmed
>
> 1½ cups coleslaw mix or combination of shredded cabbage and shredded carrots

1. Heat oven to 350°F. Combine all meatball ingredients in large bowl; mix lightly but thoroughly. Shape into 24 (1½-inch) meatballs; arrange on rack of broiler pan.

2. Bake 20 to 25 minutes or until no longer pink in centers (170°F for turkey; 160°F for beef).

3. To prepare wraps, spread plum sauce on flour tortilla; add about ¼ cup coleslaw mix and 4 hot meatballs. Fold sides of tortilla to center, overlapping edges; fold bottom and top of tortilla under, completely enclosing filling. Repeat with remaining ingredients. Cut wraps in half to serve.

Makes 6 servings

Hoisin-Orange Chicken Wraps

½ teaspoon grated orange peel
¼ cup orange juice
¼ cup hoisin sauce
8 whole Boston lettuce leaves
2 cups shredded coleslaw mix
2 cups diced cooked chicken (about 8 ounces)
Black pepper

1. Combine orange peel, juice and hoisin sauce in small bowl.

2. Arrange lettuce leaves on large serving platter. Place ¼ cup coleslaw mix, ¼ cup chicken and 1 tablespoon hoisin mixture on each leaf. Sprinkle with pepper. Fold lettuce over filling to create wrap.

Makes 4 servings

Asian Grilled Steak

¾ cup WISH-BONE® Italian Dressing*
3 tablespoon soy sauce
3 tablespoon firmly packed brown sugar
½ teaspoon ground ginger (optional)
1 (1- to 1½-pound) flank, top round or sirloin steak

Also terrific with WISH-BONE® Robusto Italian, Light Italian or Red Wine Vinaigrette Dressing.

Combine all ingredients except steak in small bowl. Pour ½ cup marinade over steak in large, shallow nonaluminum baking dish or resealable plastic bag. Cover, or close bag, and marinate in refrigerator, turning occasionally, 30 minutes or up to 24 hours. Refrigerate remaining marinade.

Remove steak from marinade, discarding marinade. Grill or broil steak, turning once and brushing frequently with reserved marinade, until steak reaches desired doneness. Let stand 10 minutes; thinly slice and serve.

Makes 4 servings

Prep Time: 5 minutes
Marinate Time: 3 hours
Cook Time: 15 minutes

Fortune Cookies

Nonstick cooking spray
2 egg whites
⅓ cup all-purpose flour
⅓ cup sugar
1 tablespoon water
¼ teaspoon vanilla
12 paper fortunes

1. Preheat oven to 400°F. Spray cookie sheets with cooking spray.

2. Whisk egg whites in small bowl until foamy. Add flour, sugar, water and vanilla; whisk until smooth.

3. Working in batches of 2, place 2 teaspoons batter on prepared cookie sheet for each cookie. Spread batter evenly with back of spoon to 3-inch round. Spray with cooking spray. Bake 4 minutes or until edges are golden brown.

4. Working quickly, remove cookies from cookie sheet and invert onto work surface. Place fortune in centers. Fold cookies in half, pressing on seam. Fold in half again, pressing to hold together. Cool completely.

5. Repeat steps 3 and 4 with remaining batter and fortunes.

Makes 1 dozen cookies

Sesame Hoisin Beer-Can Chicken

1 can (12 ounces) beer, divided
½ cup hoisin sauce
2 tablespoons honey
1 tablespoon soy sauce
1 teaspoon chili garlic sauce
½ teaspoon dark sesame oil
1 whole chicken (3½ to 4 pounds)

1. Prepare grill for indirect cooking. Combine 2 tablespoons beer, hoisin sauce, honey, soy sauce, chili garlic sauce and sesame oil in small bowl. Gently loosen skin of chicken over breast meat, legs and thighs. Spoon some hoisin mixture under skin. Pour off beer until can is two-thirds full. Hold chicken upright with opening of cavity pointing down. Insert beer can into cavity.

2. Stand chicken upright on can over drip pan. Spread legs slightly to help support chicken. Cover; grill 30 minutes over medium indirect heat. Brush chicken with remaining hoisin mixture. Cover; grill 45 to 60 minutes or until chicken is cooked through (165°F). Use metal tongs to transfer chicken to cutting board; let rest, standing up, 5 minutes. Carefully remove beer can and discard. Carve chicken and serve.

Makes 2 to 4 servings

Asian Glazed Short Ribs

4 pounds beef short ribs
1 envelope LIPTON® RECIPE SECRETS® Onion Soup Mix
½ cup apricot preserves
½ cup chili sauce
¼ cup firmly packed light brown sugar
¼ cup soy sauce
2 tablespoons apple cider vinegar
1 tablespoon cornstarch
1 cup water

Slow Cooker Directions

1. In slow cooker, arrange ribs. Combine LIPTON® RECIPE SECRETS® Onion Soup Mix with remaining ingredients, except cornstarch and water.

2. Cook, covered, on LOW 8 to 10 hours or on HIGH 4 to 6 hours or until ribs are tender.

3. Remove ribs to serving platter; keep warm. In small bowl, combine cornstarch with water. Stir into sauce and cook, covered, 10 to 15 minutes or until thickened. Pour sauce over ribs.

Makes 4 servings

Golden Gate Chinese Chicken and Cabbage Sesame Salad

1½ **pounds boneless, skinless chicken breast**
1½ **teaspoons salt-free lemon pepper**
¼ **teaspoon salt**
8 **cups thinly sliced Napa cabbage**
1 **medium-size red bell pepper, cut into julienned strips**
1 **medium-size yellow bell pepper, cut into julienned strips**
½ **cup diagonally sliced green onions**
½ **cup sesame seeds, toasted***
½ **cup chopped dried apricots**
1 **tablespoon plus ½ teaspoon grated fresh ginger, divided**
¼ **cup low-sodium chicken broth**
¼ **cup seasoned rice vinegar**
¼ **cup low-sodium soy sauce**
2 **tablespoons sugar**
2 **tablespoons dark sesame oil**
6 **Napa cabbage leaves**
1½ **cups chow mein noodles**

To toast sesame seeds, place in small skillet. Cook over medium-high heat 1 to 3 minutes or until lightly browned, stirring constantly. Remove from heat.

Place chicken in microwave-safe dish; sprinkle with lemon pepper and salt. Cover with wax paper and microwave on HIGH 8 to 10 minutes or until no longer pink in center, rotating dish half turn every 2 minutes. Or poach chicken.** Remove chicken from dish. Cool; discard liquid. Shred chicken into bite-size pieces. Combine chicken, sliced cabbage, red pepper, yellow pepper, green onions, sesame seeds, apricots and 1 tablespoon ginger in large bowl. Toss well; cover and refrigerate until ready to serve.

Combine broth, vinegar, soy sauce, sugar, oil and remaining ½ teaspoon ginger in small jar with lid; shake well. Pour over chicken and cabbage mixture; toss gently. Spoon onto individual plates lined with cabbage leaves. Sprinkle evenly with chow mein noodles. Serve immediately.

Makes 6 servings

**To poach chicken, place chicken breasts in saucepan; sprinkle with lemon pepper and salt. Cover with water. Simmer until no longer pink in center.

Favorite recipe from **National Chicken Council**

Oriental Salad Supreme

¼ **cup peanut or vegetable oil**

¼ **cup rice vinegar**

2 **tablespoons packed brown sugar**

1 **medium unpeeled cucumber, halved lengthwise and sliced**

6 **cups torn romaine or leaf lettuce**

1 **cup chow mein noodles**

¼ **cup peanuts or coarsely chopped cashews (optional)**

1. Combine oil, vinegar and brown sugar in small bowl; whisk until sugar dissolves. Toss with cucumbers. Cover; marinate in refrigerator up to 4 hours.

2. Toss cucumber and marinade with lettuce, noodles and peanuts, if desired, in large serving bowl.

Makes 4 servings

Green Tea Lychee Frappé

1 can (15 ounces) lychees in syrup,* undrained
2 cups water
2 slices peeled fresh ginger (¼ inch thick, 2 inches wide)
3 green tea bags

*Canned lychees are readily available in either the canned fruit or ethnic foods section of most large supermarkets.

1. Drain lychees, reserving syrup. Place lychees in single layer in medium resealable food storage bag; freeze until frozen. Cover syrup; refrigerate.

2. Heat water and ginger in small saucepan over medium-high heat until water is boiling. Pour over tea bags in teapot or 2-cup heatproof measuring cup; steep 3 minutes. Discard ginger and tea bags. Cover tea; refrigerate until cool.

3. Place frozen lychees, chilled green tea and ½ cup reserved syrup in blender. Blend about 20 seconds until smooth. Serve immediately.

Makes 2 servings

tip

A lychee is a subtropical fruit grown in China, Mexico and the United States. It is a small oval fruit with a rough, bright red hull. Beneath the hull is milky white flesh surrounding a single seed. The flesh is sweet and juicy. The fresh lychee is a delicacy in China. They are available fresh at Asian markets in the United States in early summer.

Sesame Chicken Slaw

6 Tyson® Fresh Boneless Skinless Chicken Thighs
4 tablespoons teriyaki marinade, divided
3 tablespoons lime juice
2 tablespoons sugar
3 tablespoons vegetable oil, divided
4 cups shredded cabbage
½ cup shredded carrots
½ cup chopped green onion tops
½ cup julienned red bell pepper
2 teaspoons sesame seeds

1. Wash hands. Cut chicken into bite-sized pieces. Wash hands. Combine 2 tablespoons teriyaki marinade, lime juice, sugar and 2 tablespoons vegetable oil in small bowl. Set aside.

2. Heat remaining 1 tablespoon vegetable oil in large nonstick skillet over medium-high heat. Add chicken and cook 3 minutes. Add remaining 2 tablespoons teriyaki marinade to chicken; stir-fry about 8 minutes or until liquid is reduced, chicken is glazed and internal juices of chicken run clear. (Or insert instant-read meat thermometer into thickest part of chicken. Temperature should read 180°F.) Remove from heat. Stir in reserved teriyaki mixture.

3. Combine cabbage, carrots and green onions in large serving bowl. Drain sauce from chicken and pour over slaw; toss to mix well. Top slaw with chicken. Garnish with bell pepper. Sprinkle with sesame seeds. Serve immediately. Refrigerate leftovers immediately.   *Makes 4 to 6 servings*

Prep Time: 10 minutes
Cook Time: 11 minutes
Total Time: 21 minutes

Chinese Almond Cookies

1 package (about 18 ounces) yellow cake mix
5 tablespoons butter, melted
1 egg
1½ teaspoons almond extract
30 whole almonds
1 egg yolk
1 teaspoon water

1. Beat cake mix, butter, egg and extract in large bowl with electric mixer at medium speed until well blended. Shape dough into ball; wrap in plastic wrap and chill 4 hours or overnight.

2. Preheat oven to 350°F. Spray cookie sheets with nonstick cooking spray; set aside.

3. Shape dough into 1-inch balls; place 2 inches apart on prepared cookie sheets. Press 1 almond into center of each ball, flattening slightly.

4. Whisk egg yolk and water in small bowl. Brush tops of cookies with egg yolk mixture. Bake 10 to 12 minutes or until lightly browned. Cool 5 minutes on cookie sheets. Remove to wire rack; cool completely.

Makes 2½ dozen cookies

Prep Time: 15 minutes
Chill Time: 4 hours
Bake Time: 10 minutes

Szechuan Chicken Tenders

2 tablespoons soy sauce

1 tablespoon chili sauce

1 tablespoon dry sherry

2 cloves garlic, minced

¼ teaspoon red pepper flakes

16 chicken tenders (about 1 pound)

1 tablespoon peanut oil

　Hot cooked rice (optional)

1. Combine soy sauce, chili sauce, sherry, garlic and red pepper flakes in shallow dish. Add chicken; toss to coat.

2. Heat oil in large nonstick skillet over medium heat. Add chicken; cook 6 minutes, turning once, until chicken is browned and no cooked through. Serve chicken with rice, if desired.　　*Makes 4 servings*

Tip: If you can take the heat, try adding a few Szechuan peppers to the dish. They are best if heated in a skillet over a low flame for a few minutes beforehand.

Acknowledgments

The publisher would like to thank the companies and associations listed below for the use of their recipes in this publication.

ACH Food Companies, Inc.

Dole Food Company, Inc.

Jennie-O Turkey Store, LLC

©2010 Kraft Foods, KRAFT, KRAFT Hexagon Logo, PHILADELPHIA AND PHILADELPHIA Logo are registered trademarks of Kraft Foods Holdings, Inc. All rights reserved.

Lee Kum Kee®

National Chicken Council / US Poultry & Egg Association

National Honey Board

National Pork Board

The Quaker® Oatmeal Kitchens

Riviana Foods Inc.

Tyson Foods, Inc.

Unilever

187

Index

Index

Metric Conversion Chart

VOLUME MEASUREMENTS (dry)

1/8 teaspoon	= 0.5 mL
1/4 teaspoon	= 1 mL
1/2 teaspoon	= 2 mL
3/4 teaspoon	= 4 mL
1 teaspoon	= 5 mL
1 tablespoon	= 15 mL
2 tablespoons	= 30 mL
1/4 cup	= 60 mL
1/3 cup	= 75 mL
1/2 cup	= 125 mL
2/3 cup	= 150 mL
3/4 cup	= 175 mL
1 cup	= 250 mL
2 cups = 1 pint	= 500 mL
3 cups	= 750 mL
4 cups = 1 quart	= 1 L

VOLUME MEASUREMENTS (fluid)

1 fluid ounce (2 tablespoons) = 30 mL
4 fluid ounces (1/2 cup) = 125 mL
8 fluid ounces (1 cup) = 250 mL
12 fluid ounces (1 1/2 cups) = 375 mL
16 fluid ounces (2 cups) = 500 mL

WEIGHTS (mass)

1/2 ounce	= 15 g
1 ounce	= 30 g
3 ounces	= 90 g
4 ounces	= 120 g
8 ounces	= 225 g
10 ounces	= 285 g
12 ounces	= 360 g
16 ounces = 1 pound	= 450 g

DIMENSIONS

1/16 inch	= 2 mm
1/8 inch	= 3 mm
1/4 inch	= 6 mm
1/2 inch	= 1.5 cm
3/4 inch	= 2 cm
1 inch	= 2.5 cm

OVEN TEMPERATURES

250°F	= 120°C
275°F	= 140°C
300°F	= 150°C
325°F	= 160°C
350°F	= 180°C
375°F	= 190°C
400°F	= 200°C
425°F	= 220°C
450°F	= 230°C

BAKING PAN SIZES

Utensil	Size in Inches/Quarts	Metric Volume	Size in Centimeters
Baking or	8×8×2	2 L	20×20×5
Cake Pan	9×9×2	2.5 L	23×23×5
(square or	12×8×2	3 L	30×20×5
rectangular)	13×9×2	3.5 L	33×23×5
Loaf Pan	8×4×3	1.5 L	20×10×7
	9×5×3	2 L	23×13×7
Round Layer	8×1½	1.2 L	20×4
Cake Pan	9×1½	1.5 L	23×4
Pie Plate	8×1¼	750 mL	20×3
	9×1¼	1 L	23×3
Baking Dish	1 quart	1 L	—
or Casserole	1½ quart	1.5 L	—
	2 quart	2 L	—